GALAXY OF SUPERSTARS

Ben Affleck

Backstreet Boys

Brandy

Garth Brooks

Mariah Carey

Matt Damon

Cameron Diaz

Celine Dion

Leonardo DiCaprio

Tom Hanks

Hanson

Jennifer Love Hewitt

Lauryn Hill

Jennifer Lopez

Ricky Martin

Ewan McGregor

Mike Myers

'N Sync

LeAnn Rimes

Adam Sandler

Britney Spears

Spice Girls

Jonathan Taylor Thomas

Venus Williams

CHELSEA HOUSE PUBLISHERS

GALAXY OF SUPERSTARS

'N Sync

John F. Grabowski

CHELSEA HOUSE PUBLISHERS
Philadelphia

Frontis: *Clockwise from top left, the quintet of 'N Sync—Justin, Chris, J.C., Lance, and Joey—are the pop-music sensation of the late 1990s.*

Produced by
21st Century Publishing and Communications, Inc.
New York, New York
http://www.21cpc.com

CHELSEA HOUSE PUBLISHERS

Editor in Chief: Stephen Reginald
Managing Editor: James D. Gallagher
Production Manager: Pamela Loos
Art Director: Sara Davis
Director of Photography: Judy L. Hasday
Senior Production Editor: LeeAnne Gelletly
Publishing Coordinator/Project Editor: James McAvoy
Assistant Editor: Anne Hill
Cover Designer: Keith Trego

Front Cover Photo: Anthony Cutajar/London Features Int'l
Back Cover Photo: Jen Lowery/London Features Int'l

The Chelsea House World Wide Web address is
http://www.chelseahouse.com

5 7 9 8 6 4

Library of Congress Cataloging-in-Publication Data

Grabowski, John F.
  'N Sync / John F. Grabowski.
     p.   cm. – (Galaxy of superstars)
  Includes bibliographical references (p.   ) and index.
  Summary: Provides background on the five individual members of the popular boy band, 'N Sync, and discusses the recent success of this group.
  ISBN 0-7910-5493-4 (hc). — ISBN 0-7910-5494-2 (pb)
  1. 'N Sync (Musical group)—Juvenile literature. 2. Singers —United States— Biography—Juvenile literature. [1. 'N Sync (Musical group). 2. Singers.]
  I. Title. II. Series.
  ML3930.N3G73   1999
  782.42184'092'2—dc21
  [b]   99—40636
                                                               CIP
                                                               AC

CONTENTS

CHAPTER 1
DISNEY IN CONCERT   7

CHAPTER 2
THE BOYS OF 'N SYNC   13

CHAPTER 3
PRACTICE MAKES PERFECT   25

CHAPTER 4
A SMASH HIT IN EUROPE   31

CHAPTER 5
BACK IN THE USA   39

CHAPTER 6
1999 AND BEYOND   49

CHRONOLOGY   59
ACCOMPLISHMENTS   60
FURTHER READING   61
INDEX   62

1

DISNEY
IN CONCERT

Being successful in show business, as in any field, is a combination of talent, hard work, and luck. The five young men known as 'N Sync—Chris Kirkpatrick, J.C. Chasez, Joey Fatone, Lance Bass, and Justin Timberlake—always had confidence in their talent. In the three years since Chris had formed the group in 1995, the boys had spent all their spare time fine-tuning their skills, practicing their singing and dancing for countless hours, day after day, week after week, month after month.

Their diligence had already paid off in spectacular fashion. They signed a contract with BMG, one of the largest record companies in the world, and became a major hit in Germany. All across Europe, Asia, and Australia, thousands of fans flocked to see 'N Sync. With their clean good looks and singing and dancing abilities, the fabulous five were one of the most engaging acts to hit the pop scene in years.

Despite their immense European popularity, however, the boys had yet to make a splash in their homeland.

Disney's Magic Kingdom is in Orlando, entertainment capital of Florida. Orlando is also the home base of 'N Sync. Already popular in Europe, the young singers and dancers gained nationwide fans in America when they performed for the Disney In Concert *television series.*

Europe was at the forefront of the "boy band" phenomenon. The Backstreet Boys, to whom 'N Sync was often compared, had only recently begun to make a name for itself in the United States. Backstreet Boys had also enjoyed early success in Germany.

The time seemed right for 'N Sync to break into the American market. The quintet's first single, "I Want You Back," was released in February of 1998. The song received a great deal of play on radio stations across the country and won the group many fans, particularly among teenage girls. The fact that the five young men were all attractive, as well as talented, did not hurt their chances. However, as Lou Pearlman of Trans Continental Entertainment says, "You have to be able to sing first or it doesn't matter how good-looking you are."

The group's first album was released soon after the single, and it too had all the earmarks of a hit. The boys began playing shows around the United States and had just finished a concert at the Mall of America in Minneapolis, Minnesota. 'N Sync was on a roll. The guys' music was catching on, and they were gathering new fans everywhere they performed.

Now, an unexpected bit of luck came their way. The Backstreet Boys had been scheduled to film a *Disney in Concert* special for the Disney Channel. The concert, to be filmed over the Memorial Day weekend at the Disney-MGM Studios, was to coincide with the opening of Animal Kingdom at Walt Disney World in Orlando, Florida.

Plans do not always work out as expected, however. The Backstreet Boys canceled at the last moment, and 'N Sync was invited to fill

in. The boys jumped at the chance. It was a tremendous opportunity for the group, which had made Orlando its base of operations.

On the Friday before the concert, the studio treated the boys and their families to a tour of the newest Disney attraction, followed by a press conference with members of the media at the Rainforest Cafe. Next, the five gave an interview for the Disney Channel. Afterwards, the boys had some free time to enjoy the park with their families before going home to rest up for the next day's performance. They took in the safari ride and the "Countdown to

As one of the hottest pop groups, the young men of 'N Sync combine their mellow harmonizing with dancing and exuberant gestures to thrill audiences worldwide.

Extinction" in Disney's latest spectacle.

Saturday began with a ceremony in which the boys set their handprints in cement in Disney's Walk of Fame. This ritual is a takeoff of the famous attraction outside Mann's Chinese Theater in Hollywood, California, but in Orlando it features entertainers who have connections with Disney.

Another press conference followed in the Beauty and the Beast Amphitheater, this one for 'N Sync's fans. Knowing how important their fans were to their success, the boys went out of their way to accommodate their admirers whenever possible. When one brave fan asked, "Today's my friend's birthday. Can you sing 'Happy Birthday' to her?" the boys did not miss a beat. They immediately chimed in with an impromptu version of "Happy Birthday to You," treating the young girl to a birthday memory she will undoubtedly cherish for years to come.

The five boys spent the remainder of the time in last-minute preparations for the concert. As they performed, mixing in songs from their album with some new arrangements, they did not disappoint their audience. Energized by the large crowd, the five put on one of their best shows, harmonizing and dancing, and their fans loved every minute of it.

By the time the evening was over, Chris, Joey, J.C., Justin, and Lance knew the concert had been a success. They did not realize just how much of a success, however. "Even after we filmed it," recalled Chris, "we just thought it was a little concert. I was like, 'Well, that was cool. Now we gotta go work on our careers.'"

On July 18, the show was televised on the Disney Channel as part of the *In Concert* series. Other shows in the series, featuring performers such as LeAnn Rimes and Brandy, had done very well, but 'N Sync received the highest ratings of all. Because of popular demand, the show was repeated several times.

The exposure brought the group countless numbers of new fans. Appearing on television could truly be said to have put them over the top. Those familiar with the boys' singing talents had their first exposure to the group's dancing prowess. Candid footage of the five and their families was included in the show, giving viewers the opportunity to get to know them a little more intimately.

Because of the Disney show, 'N Sync was no longer just a name on a CD label. The band was now a group of five likable young men ready to make their mark in their homeland, just as they already had in countries around the globe. They were talented, hip young singers and dancers who could thrill fans of all ages with their dancing abilities onstage as well as with their vocal talents. The boys had created a group with whom millions of fans the world over are "in sync."

2

THE BOYS
OF 'N SYNC

Looking back on it now, it does not seem surprising that Christopher "Chris" Alan Kirkpatrick was the inspiration for the musical group 'N Sync. Coming into the world in the small town of Clarion, Pennsylvania, on October 17, 1971, Chris was the first child born to a family with a long musical tradition. His mom, Beverly, and her brothers, sister, parents, and grandparents were all involved with music in one way or another. As she relates, "Everyone in my family is a musician. So saying that you want to put together a band in my family is a lot like telling somebody you want to learn to ride a bike in someone else's family. It's real normal."

Young Chris revealed his talent at a very early age. His mother used to sing the hymn "Coventry Carol" to put him to sleep at night when he was an infant. One day she overheard him mimicking the tune, although he was too young to speak the words.

Chris's dad died when the boy was still young, and his mom remarried. When the family moved to Dayton,

---

Chris Kirkpatrick displayed musical talent from an early age, singing, playing piano and guitar, and appearing in school musical productions. Determined to pursue a musical career, he performed at Universal Studios in Orlando, where he got the idea for the a cappella group 'N Sync.

Ohio, Chris became involved in school stage productions. He began taking piano as well as guitar and voice lessons in an effort to develop his musical talents. He also earned a reputation as one of the funniest kids in school, willing to do anything for a laugh. Chris once gave a moving performance in his high school's production of *South Pacific*. When it was time to take his bow, he walked out on the stage— in a hula skirt and coconut bra!

In addition to being serious about his music, Chris was also serious about his studies. After graduating from high school, he moved on to Valencia College in Dayton to continue his education. Although he began by majoring in theater, he soon switched over to music and psychology. When Chris was not attending classes, he sang with the school choir and also performed with groups at coffeehouses in the Dayton area.

After earning his associate of arts degree, Chris made a decision that would have a major impact on his life. Determined to get his bachelor's degree, he moved to Florida to attend Rollins College. Money soon became a problem, however, and the young student found work singing with a group called the Caroling Company. Through some members of the group, he heard that auditions were being held for the chance to perform at Universal Studios in Orlando.

This was the opportunity Chris was looking for. He passed the audition with flying colors and landed a part with the Hollywood High Tones (his name was Spike), a doo-wop group. "We used to sing outside the Fifties diner at Universal," explains Chris. "That was me—it was three guys and one girl and we'd sing

Fifties a cappella music [singing without instru-
mental accompaniment]."

Because of his job at Universal, full-time
study at Rollins was impossible. Chris had
made a decision, however, and he knew he
could only be happy by putting all his energy
into his music. After eventually dropping out
of school, he concentrated on polishing his
craft at Universal.

There were no performers in Joshua Scott
"J.C." Chasez's family, but the son of Roy and
Karen Chasez still had a great deal of expo-
sure to music. Born in Washington, D.C., on
August 8, 1976, baby Joshua loved to move to
the sounds he heard coming from the radio.
Since dancing seemed to appeal so much to
the boy, when the family moved to nearby
Bowie, Maryland, Karen signed her son up for
dance lessons.

Although the lessons helped improve the
youngster's self-confidence, he was still too
shy to perform on a stage. If it had not been for
an incident that occurred when he was 12
years old, young J.C. might never have become
the performer he is today.

One day while he was at his friend Kacy's
house, a couple of girls they knew stopped
by. The two boys had reputations as good
dancers, and the girls wanted to enter a talent
contest with them. Although reluctant at first,
J.C. agreed to go along after his friend dared
him. The foursome proceeded to take first
prize in the contest. "Even though I did it
because I was dared to," reports J.C., "I was
happy that we won. We did it a couple more
times, and wherever we went, we won first
place; we were taking all the ribbons. I just
did it for kicks."

Joshua "J.C." Chasez, an alumnus of The Mickey Mouse Club, *grew up in a family that surrounded him with music. Dedicated to his music, J.C. is known as a workaholic whose vocal talents with different musical styles help make 'N Sync's sound so special.*

Around this time, Karen Chasez spotted an item in the local newspaper that would change J.C.'s life. *The Mickey Mouse Club* (MMC) was going to be holding auditions in the Washington area. J.C. agreed to try out and was selected as one of the 12 finalists out of 500 who showed up. After further auditions in Los Angeles, J.C. was offered a job on the show. "Disney auditioned twenty thousand kids in the United States and Canada that year," says his mom. "They hired ten, and he was one of them."

J.C. moved to Orlando with his dad while his mom and younger brother and sister remained in Maryland. Over the next four years, he honed his acting and dancing skills with the show, which was also the launching pad for singer Britney Spears and actress Keri Russell of *Felicity*. In the program's weekly drama—*Emerald Cove*—he played the part of Clarence "Wipeout" Adams.

With the encouragement of his dance instructor, J.C. also began to sing and eventually performed some solos on the show. As J.C. remembers, "I didn't start singing until I got to Orlando with *The Mickey Mouse Club*. I didn't know that much about music. I just knew that I liked to dance and I started singing cover tunes." Bitten by the bug, J.C. knew he wanted to pursue his singing.

Born in Brooklyn, New York, on January 28, 1977, to Phyllis and Joseph Fatone, little Joseph Anthony Fatone Jr. liked to make believe he was Superman. As a result, his tiny body took quite a pounding. "The emergency room staff knew him by his first name," laughs his father. Luckily, Joey's attempts at singing met with more success than his attempts at flying. In this he took after his dad, Joe Sr., who once sang with a doo-wop group called the Orions.

Joey sang and danced and performed in church plays and musicals. The outgoing youngster loved the feeling he got when he performed in front of an audience. "I thought it was the greatest feeling to get applause," he explains, "to get to feed off the audience. I loved being onstage and watching people's faces. I still like getting that response."

At age seven, Joey even appeared as an

Introduced to music and theater by his parents, Joey Fatone sang and danced at Universal Studios in Orlando when he was a teenager. There he met Chris, who wanted Joey's baritone-tenor voice to enhance 'N Sync's harmonizing vocal style.

extra in the Sergio Leone film *Once Upon a Time in America*, which starred Robert De Niro. When Joey was 13 years old, his family relocated to Orlando. His talent for performing came in handy in helping him make new friends. "My family wanted to move to Florida," says Joey. "It's sunny all the time and nice. The houses were a little bit cheaper and there was actually more space."

It was in Florida that the teen improved his dancing skills through formal lessons. "In high school," says Joey, "when I tried to do musicals, that's when I pretty much got involved with dancing. I took a little bit of jazz, a little ballet, I *tried* to do tap but . . ."

Joey continued acting outside of school and appeared as an extra in *Matinee*, a 1993 film starring John Goodman. He also made a brief appearance in an episode of the television series *SeaQuest*. Despite these movie and television credits, however, Joey still got his biggest rush from performing in front of a live audience onstage.

After graduating from Orlando's Dr. Phillips High School in 1995, Joey secured a job at Universal Studios. "I did a show called *The Beetlejuice Graveyard Review*," he recalls, "and I played characters like the Wolfman and Dracula." It was the perfect position for the young performer. Where else could he get paid for doing what he enjoyed most—singing and dancing and making people happy?

Joey's love of entertaining was shared by another Universal employee with whom he had become friends, a boy by the name of Chris Kirkpatrick.

When James Lance Bass was a child, he dreamed of being an astronaut. Little did the boy realize that one day he would soar into the stratosphere in an entirely different way.

Born in Clinton, Mississippi, on May 4, 1979, to Jim and Diane Bass, Lance grew up with a love of music and gave evidence of his talent early on. As soon as he was old enough, he began singing with a children's choir. "I grew up singing in church," recalls Lance, "and I always loved singing." By the time he reached the eighth grade, he had auditioned for—and won— a spot with the Mississippi Show Stoppers, the statewide chorus. A year later, Lance began working with a voice coach in order to help him make the most of his gift.

When the chance came to join a show choir called Attache, Lance did not hesitate. He began touring the country with the group, which repeatedly won competitions, establishing a reputation as one of the best show choirs in the United States. Included in the group's repertoire were several choreographed routines. "That's where I really learned how to sing and dance," says Lance. He fell right into place and added dance lessons to his busy schedule.

For the first time in his life, Lance began to consider the field of entertainment as a possible career. The matter was clinched for him after seeing a concert that featured country singer Garth Brooks. "I was fourteen," he reports. "I thought his show was incredible. I thought, 'That's what I want to do.'"

As a senior in high school, Lance's immediate future included college. He had already been accepted at the University of Nebraska. He could not have known that his plans were about to change dramatically. College would have to wait.

Growing up in a city with a long musical heritage, it is not surprising that Justin Randall Timberlake seemed to have music in his blood. The blond, blue-eyed youngster was born to Randy and Lynn Timberlake in Memphis, Tennessee, on January 31, 1981. His father played bluegrass, so young Justin was around music all the time. "Justin has always, always exhibited great talent for music," confides his mother. "From when he was a tiny baby, not walking or talking yet,

As a boy in Clinton, Mississippi, Lance Bass loved to perform and sang and danced in show choirs. In addition to his musical talents, he brings his interest in management, describing himself as "the business one of the group."

when he was three to four months old, you could turn music on and he would always keep time with the music, kicking to the beat of the music."

While still only a toddler, Justin's parents divorced. He stayed with his mother, who eventually remarried. One constant in the youngster's early life was his participation in church activities, like other 'N Sync members. As soon as he was old enough, Justin began to sing with the other members of the congregation.

Although the youngest member of 'N Sync, Justin Timberlake is the show-business veteran of the group. He toured with local school shows, entered amateur contests, and was a performer on Star Search, *and* The Mickey Mouse Club *before teaming up with 'N Sync.*

"I come from a big background of family singers, singing in church," says Justin. "My grandmother, my daddy, my uncles, my aunts, I got it from them." As the young singer gained experience, he started entering—and winning—local talent shows, including a Dance Like the New Kids on the Block contest.

When Justin learned that the producers of

the television show *Star Search* were coming to Memphis, he jumped at the chance to audition for them. He was chosen to appear on the show, which was filmed in Orlando. Although Justin did not win *Star Search*, his trip to Florida was not a total loss. As luck would have it, *The Mickey Mouse Club* was being taped on the very next soundstage. Justin found out that in the near future the show would be holding auditions in Nashville, Tennessee, only a few hours by car from Memphis. He attended the tryouts and eventually was selected as one of the new cast members of *The Mickey Mouse Club*.

For Justin, being on the show was a dream come true. He was a big fan of the program and was thrilled to have the opportunity to perform. "By far, it's one of the best things I've ever done in my whole life," he recalls. "I couldn't have thought of a better thing to do. You get to dip your fingers into everything. You're not restricted to one thing at all. Doing the comedy was a lot of fun. You weren't restricted to one kind of music."

Justin's dream lasted two years before the show's run ended. As often happens in life, however, when one door closes, another one opens. Justin would walk through the next door together with his close friend from the show, J.C. Chasez.

PRACTICE
MAKES PERFECT

C hris Kirkpatrick formulated his plan for starting an a
cappella group in 1995, while he was working at
Universal. He contacted Justin, whom he had known from
an audition in Orlando, and Justin brought in fellow
Mickey Mouse Club alumnus J.C. When Joey, whom Chris
had come to know as a colleague at Universal (and a one-
time extra who danced the closing song on *MMC*), joined
the trio, the core of the group was in place. "Everybody
knew each other in a roundabout way," says J.C., "it was
just a matter of the order that everybody called each
other. But, Chris was the one who came up with the idea
of the group."

The boys realized they had their work cut out for them.
Thousands of groups across the country are trying to
make it in the music business, but success does not come
easily. Each of the four boys was willing to do whatever
was necessary to fulfill his dream.

They began rehearsing whenever they had free time,
usually for several hours in the evening. "When we had
no record company, no management, when we first

---

*Once 'N Sync was formed, the five boys practiced and rehearsed
for hundreds of hours, perfecting their unique vocal harmonizing
and dancing style. When they got their big break with a European
record company, the boys began their incredible rise in the pop-
music world.*

started and we were just rehearsing," relates Joey, "I was still working, and I would go to work during the day and rehearse at night, from nine to midnight. It took a lot of hard work, dedication, and some sacrifices."

Even at this early stage, the foursome, whose voices blended together perfectly, knew they were on the right track. One element was missing, however. They needed another voice for the bass parts in order to round out their sound. Where could they find someone to fill that role?

Since none of the group knew anyone he could recommend, each began making calls, including one to Justin's old vocal coach in Memphis. The coach suggested another one of his students—Lance Bass—whom the boys contacted.

Agreeing to give it a try, Lance flew to Florida and sang with the group. Right away, the others knew he was the one. "They just flew me down," remembers Lance, "and I met them and joined that day. We sang 'The Star-Spangled Banner' together, or something like that, and that was it." Lance's voice blended in perfectly, and when his parents agreed to let him join the group, the last piece of the puzzle had been put in place.

The boys knew they needed someone to oversee the group. "For the first year we were together we were struggling to find management," remembers J.C. When Justin's mom, Lynn, offered her assistance, one of the first things she did was help them decide on a name. One day, she happened to mention how "in sync" they seemed to be, since their voices and dancing blended together so well. As Lance reports, ". . . our big forte is our harmonies. That's the reason we chose 'N Sync as our name, because we love to do everything a cappella."

They later realized that 'N Sync was almost

an acronym for the last letters of their first names—N for Justin, S for Chris, Y for Joey, and C for J.C. What they still needed was another N. To make the names fit, Justin began calling Lance "Lansten," and a nickname was born.

With the group complete, the five threw themselves into their work. They spent hundreds of hours rehearsing and practicing in a hot, steamy warehouse in Orlando, where they all lived together with Justin's mom. Finally, they were ready to make their move.

At Lynn's suggestion, they put together a demo package to send to prospective managers. The package, consisting of a CD, a video, and posters, was entirely the work of the group. A friend of theirs had taped the video of the group's performances at Disney World's Pleasure Island. They invested their own money in the project. As Chris remembers, ". . . it was all done by us—the printing of the posters, the choosing of the outfits, the song orders, the choreography—everything. It was a lot of work."

In early 1996, the package reached the offices of Lou Pearlman in Orlando. Pearlman was the man who had discovered—and invested in—the Backstreet Boys, the group to whom 'N Sync would often be compared. Originally, Pearlman had been involved in the transportation field, leasing jets to acts like Michael Jackson and Paul McCartney. That initial brush with show business made him eager for more. He became an entertainment investor, financially backing acts he believed would be successful.

Pearlman liked what he heard and saw and immediately contacted his partner, Johnny Wright, who was in Germany at the time. Wright, who had previously been involved with New Kids on the Block, flew back to Orlando,

Looking like young astronauts, the boys practice their routine onstage. Appearing onstage gave the group experience in performing before live audiences and helped get their name out.

where he heard the boys sing. He was very impressed. "They could really sing," said Wright. "They had a chemistry—an aura about them. When they talked to me, they talked to me as a group, as a unit, rather than five individuals trying to pitch themselves to me— they weren't selfish."

The two men sat down with the five boys, Justin's mom, and Lance's parents. They arrived at a deal: Pearlman would supply the financial backing, and Wright would become the group's manager. 'N Sync was on its way.

Although the boys had been practicing together for several months, they still had a way to go before they were ready to sign with a record company. They continued to practice and also began appearing at small shows in the Orlando area. The five were able to try out some new dance moves they had developed while working with choreographer Robert Jacquez. One of the best in the business, Jacquez had worked with Michael Jackson, among others.

Performing in front of a live crowd also had another benefit. The boys saw the effect their vocalizing and dancing had on others, something they could not experience in a recording studio. They had always been confident in their abilities, but seeing smiling faces and hearing applause reinforced that confidence. They knew they had the talent to make others happy with their music, and that was their driving force. As Justin puts it, "I love the feeling when you're up there onstage singing and the crowd is getting into what you are doing. I love to see smiles on their faces and know that I had something to do with that."

In the meantime, Pearlman and Wright were also busy. At that time, in 1996, boy bands and pop music were not yet big in the United States. After signing on to manage the Backstreet Boys, Wright had decided to have that group make its start in the European market. His judgment proved to be on target. Backstreet Boys were a smash hit in Europe, where the Spice Girls, among others, were also filling the airways with pop music.

Wright now decided on the same plan of action for 'N Sync. With his contacts overseas, he soon had BMG in Germany ready to offer the boys a deal. The five signed contracts with BMG Ariola Munich, and within days the boys were on a plane heading for Germany. The quick turn of events did not faze the young men. As Justin recalls, "We were, like, we don't care where you take us—we just want to sing!" And, as they were to soon find out, Germany was ready to hear them.

4

A SMASH HIT
IN EUROPE

The boys were based in Munich for the next year and a half, but their travels would soon take them far and wide. The first order of business was to gather together a team of producers, songwriters, and arrangers. Johnny Wright quickly enlisted the services of producers Denniz Pop and Max Martin. In past years, this duo had teamed together with the Backstreet Boys, Robyn, and Ace of Bass. Their track record was quite impressive. Other arrangers, producers, and songwriters were enlisted, including Gary Carolla, Christian Hamm, Kristian Lundin, Veit Renn, and Full Force.

The boys flew to Stockholm, Sweden, to record two songs at Pop's Cheiron Studios. The resulting tunes— "I Want You Back" and "Tearin' Up My Heart"—would be 'N Sync's first two single releases. At the same time, others were working behind the scenes to put together the material for the group's first album. These preparations required the boys to fly back and forth to Orlando, where they recorded at Lou Pearlman's Trans Continental studio or at Parc or House of Hits studios.

Like many of the boy bands of the '90s, 'N Sync established its foothold on the pop-music world in Europe. Based in Munich, Germany, for more than a year, the boys recorded hit singles, toured the country, and received an enthusiastic reception.

'N Sync's work quickly paid off. "I Want You Back" was released in Germany in September 1996 and immediately became a hit. As J.C. would describe it, "The song is about suddenly finding yourself separated from the person you feel so deeply about because you've done something stupid to screw it up. I think it hits [people] because they can relate to it like a love song, but it's powerful and up tempo enough to kick them too." The song broke Michael Jackson's record by becoming Germany's fastest-rising single ever.

BMG President Thomas Stein marveled, "I have hardly ever witnessed newcomers enter the German charts with such incredible, rocket-like speed." Although the tune never actually reached the number one spot, it remained on the charts long enough to sell more than 350,000 copies, a phenomenal number for a country the size of Germany.

When "Tearin' Up My Heart" was released a couple of months later, it too became a hit. It reached the number 10 spot on the charts, also selling more than 350,000 copies. Staying at the top is often said to be harder than reaching it in the first place. Many groups in the past had enjoyed one hit song and were never heard from again. By following up with a second hit, 'N Sync proved it was not a one-hit wonder. The boys were developing a fan base who loved their sound and would buy future recordings. That base was fast spreading beyond Germany's borders as more songs were released—and became hits—in Austria, Holland, Hungary, Sweden, and Switzerland.

With their singles receiving increasing airtime, the plan was for the group to hit the road for a 17-date tour of Germany. 'N Sync's

popularity had reached such heights that concerts quickly sold out. Fans were anxious to get their first chance to see the boys in person.

The tour had several objectives. First, it allowed more people to hear the group's music. The more people heard 'N Sync's songs, the more likely it was that they would become fans and buy the boys' album when it was released later in the year.

Second, the tour helped fans get to know the boys themselves. By seeing them perform on stage, admirers could connect faces and personalities to the voices they were familiar with from the radio. The result, hopefully, would help audiences develop a bond with the group.

Aside from the marketing aspects, the tour would also give 'N Sync an opportunity to develop its stage act. Fans had heard how well the boys could sing. Now, they could also see how well the group could dance and perform.

The "Gang of Five" shows fans their dancing prowess. Part of what separates 'N Sync from other boy bands is their energetic action onstage.

A final reason for the tour was to give Chris, Joey, J.C., Justin, and Lance a taste of what they would face in the future. Traveling from one city to another and performing every night can be extremely tiring, and facing the media day after day can be mentally exhausting. The tour would give the boys some hint as to what their lives would be like as they became more famous.

When faced with a grueling schedule, it often helps if performers develop a routine that prepares them to face each day. During the course of the tour, the boys came up with two rituals they performed before each show. The first was a quick game of Hacky Sack to help loosen them up and ease the tension. Of course this could present other problems. "We have to delay the show sometimes," reports Lance, "because we're not very good."

The other ritual is one that helps the group prepare mentally. All five of the boys have strong religious beliefs. Just prior to the start of a show, they gather together with their road crew for a moment of prayer. "Without praying," they all concur, "we wouldn't dare to take a step on the stage."

The mini-tour was a resounding success. Mobs of fans came out to see the group at every stop along the way. Young women screamed out their names whenever they appeared in public. The boys finally had to travel with bodyguards wherever they went.

Ironically, while on tour the group happened to meet up with the Spice Girls, who were largely responsible for the "pop music" wave 'N Sync was following. The encounter occurred at an airport in Germany where the two groups were waiting to catch flights. "They didn't have security and we didn't have security," recalled

Chris. "We met them in the airport and we just sat down and talked with them." The tour was just the beginning, however. In May 1997, 'N Sync's first album was ready for release. A new tour was scheduled, this one to take the boys all across the continent of Europe.

European fans could not get enough. Not only did fans have the boys' singles, but MTV Europe and Viva! (a German version of MTV) were airing videos of the group's first two hits. Their popularity on the rise, the boys were in constant demand for interviews and photo shoots. They flew from city to city, laying the groundwork for their upcoming tour.

Scheduled for release in Germany on May 26, the boys' first album, 'N Sync, had already surpassed the 250,000 mark in advance sales. 'N Sync broke into the charts at number 22 and then quickly shot up to the top position. It was the first 'N Sync recording to reach the number one spot and also made the top-10 in Austria, Holland, Hungary, Sweden, and Switzerland.

Fourteen songs were included on 'N Sync. The songs were the creations of several writers and producers and covered a wide range of styles. "I Want You Back," the up-tempo, catchy tune that was the group's first hit single, is about a ruined love affair. "Tearin' Up My Heart" is the addictive follow-up single about another frustrated relationship. "For the Girl Who Has Everything" and "Sailing" are ballads that beautifully demonstrate the boys' harmonizing talents. The latter is a remake of the Christopher Cross hit of 1980—and one of Joey's dad's favorite songs.

"More Than a Feeling" is an updated version of a 1976 hit by the group Boston. The boys sang it in their own inimitable style, and the

Adoring fans line up for autographs from their idols. The boys of 'N Sync don't hesitate to show their appreciation to their crowds of fans, who have helped make the group an international hit.

song came across as a tuneful ballad rather than the hard-rock original interpretation. That song is one of five that appeared on the European version of *'N Sync* but which would not appear on the album later released in the United States. The other four in that category are "Riddle," "Best of My Life," "Together Again," and "Forever Young." The last is not the Rod Stewart hit but rather an inspirational ditty about prevailing against all odds. "Forever Young" had a special meaning for the boys since it symbolized their own road to stardom.

The remaining songs included the sentimental love song "I Need Love," an upbeat dance tune, "You Got It", and the song "Crazy for You," which is a kind of mixture of several styles. "Here We Go," which was released as a single and would rise to number eight in Germany, is one of the most popular songs at the boys' concerts. The number is like a singalong, with the audience answering the five's cry of "Here we go" by responding, "'N Sync has got the flow!"

The album's final cut, "Giddy Up," is Chris's favorite since it was cowritten by the boys together with Veit Renn. "I can remember when we were in the studio writing that," he recalls, "and how much fun it was to write with the guys."

The many months of practice and rehearsals were well worth the effort. Backed by a seven-piece band, the boys began the tour, performing the songs from their new album, accompanied by their signature dance athletics. 'N Sync was truly a European sensation, winning the hearts of fans everywhere they performed. The tour proved to be exhausting, however. "We tour so hard," reported Justin. "We've toured for a month straight, city after city, and we'd get maybe two days off the entire tour. I had never experienced touring to the point that you started losing weight!"

Touring can also have its dangers. At one stop along the way, Justin broke his thumb during a performance. "Somebody put some water on the stage," he recalls. "We were doing an outside show and they were hosing down the audience. We do this dance move where we slide across the stage and my hand buckled."

Despite such setbacks, success continued to follow the group. When all was said and done, the results could not have been more positive. The boys' faith in themselves—and Lou Pearlman's and Johnny Wright's—had not been misplaced. With three hit singles, a smash album, and a major tour under their belts, the five headed back home to Florida for some rest and relaxation.

5

BACK IN
THE USA

The boys returned home to find a resurgence of pop music in the United States. The Spice Girls and Hanson were winning countless fans among the younger set. When the Backstreet Boys hit the charts with their single "Quit Playing Games (With My Heart)," it appeared that the country might finally be ready to accept the "boy band" craze which had taken Europe by storm.

The five also came home with new looks. Being exposed to fashions and styles in Europe gave the boys a chance to express their personalities through changes in their appearances. Chris had allowed his hair to grow and now wore a small goatee. Joey also adopted the goatee look and had his hair cut shorter on the sides. J.C.'s hair was a little longer and his clothes a little sportier. Justin's curly locks were now bleached, and he too dressed more casually. Lance's most noticeable change was getting his blond hair spiked.

Another thing that changed was the way in which the five were received. They had gotten used to being mobbed everywhere they went overseas, but they were brought

Returning from Europe with some "new looks" to show off their individuality, the boys were ready to ride the resurgent wave of enthusiasm for boy bands in the United States. They began a hectic schedule of recording and preparing for another tour overseas.

back to reality when they found they could go wherever they wanted without being recognized or mobbed. The boys realized this was a good experience. "We consider it lucky that we hit in Europe and got so huge, but remained unknown in the States," remembered Justin. "It gave us the chance to sit back and digest what was happening as it happened. We might have gotten crazy about it, but then we'd come home and it was like a reality check."

'N Sync still had other commitments, however, before it could test the American musical waters. Because of their popularity, which was spreading like wildfire, the boys were scheduled for a promotional tour overseas. Their legions of fans were no longer confined to Europe. The group now had thousands of fans in Asia and Australia who were clamoring to see their idols.

Before heading for Asia, the group appeared on television, radio, and in all the print media in Europe. When they finally performed in the Far East, the boys found fans there to be every bit as avid as those elsewhere, but much more polite. The tour ended with a stop in Australia, where the band's popularity had also been established.

From the "Land Down Under," 'N Sync returned to the United States again. Another European jaunt was planned for early 1998, however, and the five had little time for relaxation. They began working on new songs and new dance routines for their next tour. In January, the group took to the highways and byways of Europe again, serenading their fans with their new act. For two months the boys entertained their adoring admirers, who never seemed to get enough of them.

When the band returned home this time, a

pleasant surprise was waiting for them. "I Want You Back" had been released in the United States on February 13. Within weeks, it had shown signs of being as big a hit here as it had been abroad. The video was getting a lot of play on MTV, and the song was on its way. America was finding out what much of the rest of the world already knew—'N Sync was indeed a force to be reckoned with.

Some critics, however, dismissed the group as nothing more than a clone of the Backstreet Boys. Others went so far as to call 'N Sync "Backstreet Boys lite." The two groups do, in fact, have much in common. They are both composed of five talented, good-looking young men, both were based in Orlando, and both were discovered and backed by Lou Pearlman's organization.

Wildly popular in Europe, the Backstreet Boys are one of the first of the boy bands. Although often compared to Backstreet, 'N Sync is uniquely different. Each of the 'N Sync five gives his own vocal sound to the group's melodious harmonizing, and their acrobatic dance moves also set them apart.

The boys and their fans, however, have learned not to worry about such negative notions. They view their dancing talents as one important difference between the two groups. "I think the choreography is really key," says Chris. "When you see our show, you'll see that we dance with every song—except for one a cappella song. When we sing, we like to dance, we like to move around and we show that onstage. There's even a dance break where all we do is dance. It's a lot of fun."

"I Want You Back" remained on the charts for six months, making it all the way up to number 13. The song sold more than a million copies and gave the boys memories they would never forget. "I heard the song on the radio on *Casey's Top 40*," Lance would later remark, "and it was weird, because we all grew up listening to Casey Kasem. It sounded so good!"

'N Sync was released by RCA Records a little more than a month after "I Want You Back" hit the stores. The album broke into *Billboard's* top 200 chart at number 40 and began its rise toward the top 10. As summer came, the album had sold more than a million copies and gone platinum. The American version of *'N Sync* included four songs not on the European release. "I Just Wanna Be with You" was the work of producers Full Force. A little funkier than most of the group's work, the song included a sample from Sly and the Family Stone's classic "Family Affair." "Everything I Own" was the boys' rendition of the 1970s soft-rock hit by Bread, while "I Drive Myself Crazy," later released as a single in Germany, was a soulful mixture of rhythm-and-blues and pop.

The last new track on the album was Justin's and Lance's favorite. "God Must Have Spent a

Little More Time on You" is a beautiful romantic ballad that would be the group's third single
released in the States. As Lance put it, ". . .
the words and melody are incredible. I get chill
bumps whenever I listen to it."

'N Sync fans with personal computers had
an additional surprise in store for them. *'N Sync*
is actually an enhanced CD, with several features that can be viewed on a computer. When
the disc is inserted into a computer's CD-ROM
drive, files can be opened that present bio-
graphical information about the boys, list
lyrics to the songs, and connect the user with
websites on the Internet. Users can also view
pictures and even a brief video.

Over the next several weeks, the boys spent
time on the road promoting the album and
getting ready for their first American tour. The
group's first concert of note was at the Mall of
America in Minneapolis, but the five's break-
through date was at Walt Disney World in
Orlando. When the Disney concert was broad-
cast on the Disney Channel that summer, the
'N Sync phenomenon truly took off.

Following the Disney concert, the boys ven-
tured to New York City for the first time. The
highlight of the trip to the Big Apple was a
concert sponsored by radio station Z100 to
raise money for charity. Staged at New York's
legendary Radio City Music Hall, the concert
included such performers as Mariah Carey,
Gloria Estefan, Olivia Newton-John, Paula Cole,
Third Eye Blind, and Matchbox 20. As the
review in *Billboard* reported, 'N Sync held its
own. "Among favorite moments for the sold-
out Radio City Music Hall crowd [was] . . . a
performance by 'N Sync, who danced and sang
like banshees amid throngs of mesmerized

The members of 'N Sync entertain enthusiastic fans at a charity concert run by Z100 in New York City. All of the guys enjoy performing at benefits, believing that it is important to give of their time and talents to help others.

and screaming girls."

The rest of the summer of '98 found the boys stepping up their hectic pace. They continued to make promotional appearances at stores, giving their fans a chance to meet them at every stop along the way. The media blitz snowballed as magazines such as *Billboard, Entertainment Weekly, Teen People, Seventeen, Teen Beat, Twist,* and *Tiger Beat* all clamored for interviews and photos. The boys' schedule of concert appearances took them north to Canada, where their fans were eager to have the chance to see them in person for the first time.

In August the five were back in the United

States performing at arenas, theme parks, state fairs, and malls. 'N Sync did not forget TV, either. The group was booked for appearances on both *The Tonight Show with Jay Leno* and *Live! With Regis & Kathie Lee.*

One of the boys' favorite kinds of performances were their charity concerts, such as the one run by Z100 in New York. "I think you just do as much as you can," said Chris to *Teen Beat* magazine. "When I was little, I tried to do as much as I could as often as I could. Now that we've got a name out there, it's a lot easier for us to do more for charity because you can appeal to the masses."

'N Sync headlined at the event called The Truth Train, on their home territory in Florida. This event, organized by Students Working Against Tobacco, tried to bring attention to the problem of teen smoking. Another concert in California was the Wango Tango benefit, which raised money for local organizations. "We played in a stadium and it was a huge rush to be on that stage in front of that many people," said J.C. "There was a good vibe because it was for a good cause too, so we enjoyed it."

As the summer neared its end, the boys made another promotional trip to New York. Entertainment mogul Richard Branson was opening a new Virgin Megastore in downtown Manhattan at the edge of Greenwich Village. 'N Sync was enlisted, along with other celebrities, to take part in the festivities. The highlight of the day was a double-decker bus ride from Times Square to the downtown store. Together with Branson, singer Petula Clark, and camera crews, the boys waved to fans and sang from the upper level of the bus as it moved through the streets of the city. Some lucky fans along

Crowds gather to watch and cheer as the boys ride through New York City to the opening of Virgin Records' megastore in downtown Manhattan.

the way were allowed to board the bus and meet their idols. It was the kind of opportunity the boys enjoyed—a chance to give a little something back to their fans.

Eventually, the boys returned home, but they found little time to rest up and relax. Over the next two weeks they recorded the vocals for 14 songs that were to be featured on their new album, due to be released in November. Their second album—*Home for Christmas*—consisted of a few old standards and some new Christmas tunes. Included among the traditional songs were "The First Noel," "O Holy Night," and the Mel Torme classic "The Christmas Song (Chestnuts Roasting on an Open Fire)."

The new holiday songs, many of which were produced by Veit Renn, included "Home for Christmas," "Under My Tree," "I Never Knew the Meaning of Christmas," "Merry Christmas, Happy Holidays," "I Guess It's Christmas Time," "All I Want Is You This Christmas," "In Love on Christmas," "It's Christmas," "Love's in Our Hearts on Christmas Day," "The Only Gift," and "Kiss Me at Midnight."

Home for Christmas was scheduled for release just prior to the start of their headlining tour. Before that, however, the boys would be spending two weeks performing as the opening act for Janet Jackson's *Velvet Rope* tour. This was a huge thrill for the group, especially for young Justin. "You don't understand how much I'm in love with Janet Jackson," he said. "Probably about two or three years ago I had her on my wall, so I'm pretty infatuated."

When November 10 rolled around, *Home for Christmas* hit the stores and immediately took off on the charts, making its first appearance on the *Billboard* charts at number seven. Meanwhile, *'N Sync* was still on the charts at number three. Incredibly, the boys had two albums in the top 10 at the same time! This almost unheard-of event proved beyond the shadow of a doubt what the group's fans already knew: the band that had smashed records in Europe was destined to be as big, if not bigger, in the United States. It was only a matter of time.

6

1999 AND
BEYOND

As the end of 1998 approached, Chris, J.C., Joey, Lance, and Justin had a couple of weeks to reflect on all that had happened in an amazing year. They took a break from their tour to return home and spend the Christmas holidays with their families. Looking back, it was difficult to grasp just how far 'N Sync had come in such a short time.

At the beginning of the year, the group was still largely unknown in the United States. The boys could walk around without having to worry about being besieged by fans wherever they went. Now, 12 months later, the five were being hailed as the best new group of the year.

The video for their hit single "I Want You Back" had won two *Billboard* Music Video Awards for them—as Best Clip of the Year and Best New Artist Clip of the Year in the dance-video category. They had two hit singles under their belts and two albums in the top 10. Amazingly, "God Must Have Spent a Little More Time on You" was receiving so much playing time on the radio that it had

The year 1999 was a triumph for the boys of 'N Sync, shown here with one of their media awards. Hailed as the hottest new group of the year, their U.S. tour was a tremendous success. They were recording songs, winning awards, and television shows clamored for them. The future looked even brighter for the five young men who only want to be one thing: "'N Sync."

climbed to number 34 on the singles chart. (It would later be released as a single.)

Television had not forgotten the group, either. In the month of December alone, the boys were welcome guests on *Live! With Regis & Kathie Lee* and visited with *CBS This Morning*. Specials on which they appeared that month included *Holiday in Concert*, *A Kathie Lee Christmas*, and *Walt Disney World's Very Merry Christmas Parade*.

'N Sync's headlining trek capped the year and would begin the new one of 1999. Following the holiday break, the boys resumed touring in Minnesota before heading west later in January. On another break in February, they worked on their next album. Returning to the road once again in March and April, the group toured with Tatyana Ali.

May 1999 began with new confirmation of the boys' popularity when 'N Sync was honored with the accolade Favorite Group in voting by more than six million kids for Nickelodeon's 12th Annual Kids' Choice Awards. The boys also performed on the show, which was hosted by television personality Rosie O'Donnell.

That same month the group was honored in another, more unusual, way. On May 2, the Caribbean islands of St. Vincent and the Grenadines issued a postage stamp featuring the boys' likenesses. Although most countries do not issue stamps depicting living persons, the island nations are among the few that do.

According to the postmaster of St. Vincent, other entertainers have been depicted in the past. The boys were chosen because they "represented the best of what art and entertainment can present to young people, as they are positive role models with a positive message."

Don't plan on buying the stamps to use on your Christmas cards, however. These special issues, costing one Caribbean dollar each, can only be used on letters or cards mailed from St. Vincent and the Grenadines.

What does the remainder of 1999, and the more distant future, hold for Chris, J.C., Joey, Lance, and Justin? Concert dates were scheduled to fill most of the summer months

In a daring performance at the annual Blockbuster Entertainment Awards in mid-1999, the five thrilled fans when wires lifted them into the air. The ceremony also honored the boys with the Favorite New Group Award.

as the *Boys of Summer* tour made its way across the United States and Canada. Fellow boy band Five and former New Kid on the Block Jordan Knight were slated to tour with 'N Sync. A first-ever trip to Brazil was also on the boys' itinerary.

The group will also continue to be seen on television. Small-screen appearances were scheduled for the *Teen Awards*, *Teenapaloosa*, *Miss Teen USA*, and the *MTV Awards*. In addition, the pay-per-view special *'N Sync 'N Concert* was to air in September.

Obviously, the boys' music is still their foremost concern. They no longer worry about being called a Backstreet Boys clone. They have their own identity, of which they are very proud. As Justin says, "We didn't want to be the next *anybody*. We wanted to be the first 'N Sync."

The group's third album, to which songwriters Diane Warren and David Foster brought their talents, was set for release in October. Both of these artists received 1998 Academy Award nominations, Warren for Aerosmith's "I Don't Want to Miss a Thing" from the film *Armageddon* and Foster for Celine Dion's "The Prayer" from *The Quest for Camelot*. In addition, Justin cowrote one of the tunes for the third album, and J.C. wrote another.

By early summer, the boys' vocal skills were also heard in collaboration with several other artists. In one such partnership, they were to sing backup vocals on the group Alabama's new song—'N Sync's own "God Must Have Spent a Little More Time on You." The track is on Alabama's *20th Century* album.

The boys also recorded a ballad—"Music of My Heart"—together with Gloria Estefan. The

song is featured on the soundtrack of the movie *Music of the Heart*, scheduled for release in the fall of 1999 and starring Meryl Streep, Aidan Quinn, and Estefan. A third project found them teaming up with Phil Collins on the soundtrack of the Disney animated feature *Tarzan*. (They can be heard on the a cappella version of "Trashin' the Camp.")

The silver screen likewise beckons the fabulous quintet. According to one source, the boys will be filming a full-length feature some time in the fall of '99. Reportedly they will be playing roles rather than portraying themselves.

And for 'N Sync fans who can never seem to get enough of the boys, another undertaking is sure to make them sit up and take notice. The group's very own PlayStation video game is on

Although music is their first love, with singles and albums hitting the charts, the boys also have personal plans beyond touring and recording. Television and films beckon, and some business enterprises appear to be in their futures.

the horizon for the near future.

Aside from their work as a group, Chris and Lance have also put in time on their own personal ventures. The boys have talked on occasion about starting their own line of clothes, and Chris has finally done something about it. His Fu-Man Skeeto clothing line, composed of his own creations, was set to debut by 2000.

Lance has gotten into the managing end of the music business, launching Free Lance Entertainment. He oversees the careers of Meredith Edwards and Jack Defeo—two new country singers trying to make their marks. Lance's mother, Diane, and sister, Stacy, head the company, while he pitches in whenever he can. "I do it at night in hotel rooms," he reports. "It's all on the phone."

With a feverish schedule such as theirs, the boys don't have much spare time. When they do, however, each has his own way of spending his downtime. Chris likes most all sports but especially football. He played in high school and says he is pretty good at it now. He also enjoys martial arts and skating. Never tiring of listening to music, Chris has fun attending other groups' concerts.

Unlike Chris, J.C. is not a sports fan. He prefers to spend his spare time with his family, and he would like to have, as he says, "more time to myself." He does enjoy going to the movies, though. It's a way, he explains, to escape from reality for a couple of hours.

In his free time, Joey likes to jet-ski, although he admits he could be better at it. As he says, ". . . I have fun just going fast and turning." He often spends his evenings either going to the movies, sleeping, or enjoying the clubs. Since as a child he was determined to be Superman, it should be no surprise that he is always on the lookout for Superman memorabilia for his large collection.

Like J.C., Lance is not much of a sports fan. He plays basketball once in while with the guys, but says he is "bad" at the game. For Lance, relaxing means enjoying his family and friends or indulging his favorite activity—a day at the beach. "I'm the biggest beach bum," he admits.

For Justin, basketball is his second love, and he plays as often as he can. He is also an avid collector of basketball gear. When not playing, he likes to "just chill" or spend time with his younger brothers.

One thing the boys don't have much time for is dating. It is hard to develop serious relationships when the five are on the road playing nearly 150 concerts a year, making promotional appearances, recording albums, and developing other projects. The boys do, however, have some definite thoughts on what they look for in a girl.

Chris, naturally, looks for a good sense of humor. A young woman who is spontaneous, adventurous, and very outgoing has the best chance of catching his eye. Chris says she should also have "a very beautiful smile. Her eyes and her smile are what say it all for me." Gwen Stefani of No Doubt is his idea of a dream girl. Although he figures he will eventually get married, Chris has no plans to settle down in the immediate future. He is having too much fun living out his dreams and playing the field.

J.C. is serious and hardworking. He never seems to have time to date. When he does

A pleasurable time for the boys of 'N Sync was lending their talents to the Miss Teen USA pageant. The guys obviously enjoy being surrounded by young women, but their hectic schedule leaves them little time for long-term relationships.

get the chance, he looks for someone who can help him relax and make him laugh. She must also be patient, however, since J.C. is extremely serious about succeeding in the music business that makes up such a large part of his life. Rather than being a party animal, like Chris, Joey, or Justin, J.C.'s idea of an enjoyable evening is a quiet, romantic dinner, possibly followed by an entertaining show. Although looks are not the most important thing to him, he does admit that the first thing he notices about a girl are her eyes and her lips.

As the most talkative and flirtatious member of the group, Joey is nicknamed "Chick Magnet" by Chris. He is attracted to young women who are friendly and confident and who can match his action on the dance floor. It also helps if a chosen one can cook; Joey has been spoiled by his mom's Italian cuisine.

One of the girls Joey has paired off with recently is Lene Crawford Nystrom, a singer in the Swedish band Aqua. "Lene is very attractive and sexy," says Joey, "and I love her sense of humor." Unfortunately, with both of them so committed to, and involved with, their respective groups, there has not yet been time for the relationship to reach the serious stage.

Always the gentleman, Lance has been nicknamed "Stealth" by the others because of the way he can quietly and quickly sweep a girl right off her feet. The sweet, innocent, wholesome, all-American girl is his ideal. She should also be the outdoors type, able to enjoy horseback riding, hiking, and the beach. If the girl is daring enough to go for something more adventurous, like parasailing, so much the better. One of the girls who has spent a good deal of time with Lance recently is Danielle Fishel, who plays the part of Topanga on *Boy Meets World*.

Like all of the others, Justin thinks personality in a girl is much more important than looks. "I like a girl with a good sense of humor, who's humble, and sensitive," says the youngest member of 'N Sync. The group's "Mr. Smooth" looks for self-confidence in his dates but not cockiness. He hopes some day to find a girl who will simply like him for *who* he is rather than *what* he is. Singer Britney Spears, a fellow *Mickey Mouse Club* alumna, is a young lady rumored to be the current love interest of the blond, curly-haired heartthrob.

What the more distant future holds for the ambitious boys still remains to be seen. All of them fully realize that fame can be a fleeting thing. "We could be gone next year," says Chris, "and people won't have a clue who we were." Having been involved in show business for several years now, there is a good possibility they may spend more time in the writing or production part of the industry. J.C. in particular often pictures himself in some behind-the-scenes capacity, such as being an engineer or producer.

Whatever the future may bring, there is one thing of which admirers can be sure: 'N Sync plans on bringing pleasure to its millions of fans for years to come, and the five will do it their way. "We want to be pioneers in the music industry," says Justin. "We want to make our own name. We have inspiration individually and as a group . . . but we just want to be 'N Sync." Millions of fans around the world could ask for nothing more.

CHRONOLOGY

1971   Christopher Alan Kirkpatrick born on October 17 in Clarion, Pennsylvania.

1976   Joshua Scott Chasez born on August 8 in Washington, D.C.

1977   Joseph Anthony Fatone Jr. born on January 28 in Brooklyn, New York.

1979   James Lance Bass born on May 4 in Clinton, Mississippi.

1981   Justin Randall Timberlake born on January 31 in Memphis, Tennessee.

1995   'N Sync formed by Chris Kirkpatrick.

1996   Johnny Wright becomes 'N Sync's manager; sign recording contract with BMG Ariola Munich, Germany; release "I Want You Back" and "Tearin' Up My Heart" in Germany; tour Germany.

1997   Release album 'N Sync in Germany; tour Europe, Asia, and Australia.

1998   Release "I Want You Back" and "Tearin' Up My Heart" in U.S.; release 'N Sync in U.S.; film In Concert Special for Disney Channel at Walt Disney World; tour U.S.; release Home for Christmas in U.S.

1999   Win two Billboard Music Video Awards, Best Clip of the Year and Best New Artist Clip of the Year; 'N Sync stamp issued by islands of St. Vincent and the Grenadines; voted Favorite Group at 12th Annual Nickelodeon's Kids' Choice Awards; tour U.S. and Canada; record third album; sign with Jive records; settle lawsuit brought against them by former manager Lou Pearlman.

2000   Release No Strings Attached, which makes history as the first album to sell more than 1 million copies in a single day; release the singles "Bye Bye Bye" and "It's Gonna Be Me"; receive two Grammy Award nominations; tour the U.S.; perform at the Academy Awards ceremony; sign endorsement deal with McDonalds; win five Teen Choice Awards; win four Billboard Awards; receive six MTV Video Music Award nominations.

2001   Win the People's Choice Award for Favorite Musical Group; win American Music Award for internet artist of the year; perform at Super Bowl XXXV half-time show; nominated for multiple Grammy Awards; www.nsync.com is the most popular music artist site on the World Wide Web.

ACCOMPLISHMENTS

Singles (U.S.)

1998   "I Want You Back"
         "Tearin' Up My Heart"
         "Merry Christmas, Happy Holidays"

1999   "God Must Have Spent a Little More Time on You"
         "Music of My Heart"

2000   "Bye Bye Bye"
         "It's Gonna Be Me"

Albums (U.S.)

1998   *'N Sync*
         Home for Christmas

2000   *No Strings Attached*

Major television appearances (U.S.)

1998   *'N Sync in Concert*
         The Late Show with David Letterman
         The Tonight Show with Jay Leno
         Live! With Regis & Kathie Lee
         CBS This Morning
         Ricki Lake
         Holiday in Concert
         Walt Disney World's Very Merry Christmas Parade
         A Kathie Lee Christmas

1999   *Nickelodeon's 12th Annual Kids' Choice Awards*

2000   *Good Morning America*
         Total Request Live
         The Rosie O'Donnell Show
         The Today Show
         'N Sync Live From Madison Square Garden
         Fox Teen Choice Awards
         MTV Video Music Awards
         Academy Awards

2001   *American Music Awards*
         Super Bowl XXXV

FURTHER READING

Golden, Anna Louise. *'N Sync: An Unauthorized Biography*. New York: St. Martin's, 1999.

Johns, Michael-Anne. *'N Sync—Backstage Pass: Your Kickin' Keepsake Scrapbook!* New York: Scholastic, 1999.

Kelman, Chris. *'N Sync*. New York: Andrews McMeel Publishing, 1999.

Krulik, Nancy E. *'N Sync with J.C.* New York: Pocket Books, 1999.

Netter, Matt. *'N Sync: Tearin' Up the Charts*. New York: Pocket Books, 1998.

Netter, Matt. *'N Sync with Justin*. New York: Pocket Books, 1999.

Nichols, Angie. *'N Sync*. London: Virgin Books, 1998.

'N Sync with K.M. Squires. *'N Sync: The Official Book*. New York: Bantam Doubleday Dell, 1998.

INDEX

Backstreet Boys, 8, 27, 29, 31, 39, 41-42

Bass, James Lance, 7, 10, 19-20, 26, 34, 42-43, 49, 54, 55, 57

"Best of My Life" (single), 36

BMG, 7, 29, 32

Boys of Summer tour, 52

Branson, Richard, 45

Chasez, Joshua Scott "J.C.", 7, 10, 15-17, 23, 25, 32, 34, 39, 49, 52, 54, 55-57, 58

Collins, Phil, 53

"Crazy for You" (single), 36

Disney in Concert (TV), 8-11, 43

Estefan, Gloria, 52, 53

"Everything I Own" (single), 42

Fatone, Joseph "Joey" Anthony, Jr., 7, 10, 17-19, 25, 26, 34, 39, 49, 54-55, 57

Fishel, Danielle, 57

"Forever Young" (single), 36

"For the Girl Who Has Everything" (single), 35

Free Lance Entertainment, 54

Full Force, 31

Fu-Man Skeeto clothing line, 54

"Giddy Up" (single), 37

"God Must Have Spent A Little More Time on You" (single), 42-43, 49-50, 52

Grenadines/St. Vincent, 50-51

"Here We Go" (single), 36-37

Home for Christmas (album), 46-47

"I Drive Myself Crazy" (single), 42

"I Just Wanna Be with You" (single), 42

"I Need Love" (single), 36

"I Want You Back" (single), 8, 31, 32, 35, 41, 42

I Want You Back (video), 41, 49

Jackson, Janet/*Velvet Rope* tour, 47

Jackson, Michael, 27

Jacquez, Robert, 29

Kirkpatrick, Christopher "Chris" Alan, 7, 10, 13-15, 25, 27, 34, 37, 39, 42, 49, 54, 55, 58

McCartney, Paul, 27

Mickey Mouse Club, The (MMC), 16-17, 23, 25, 58

"More Than a Feeling" (single), 35-36

"Music of My Heart" (soundtrack), 52-53

New Kids on the Block, 27

Nickelodeon's 12th Annual Kids' Choice Awards, 50

'N Sync
American tours of, 8, 43-46, 50, 52
Asian/Australian tour of, 7, 40
charity concerts of, 43, 45
early performances of, 28-29
European tours of, 7-8, 29, 31-37, 40
fans of, 10, 11, 32-35, 40, 42, 43, 45-46
formation of, 7, 25-29
future of, 51-58
origin of name of, 26-27
TV appearances of, 45, 50, 52

'N Sync (album), 8, 33, 35-37, 42-43, 47

'N Sync 'N Concert (TV), 52

Nystrom, Lene Crawford, 57

Pearlman, Lou, 8, 27, 28, 29, 31, 37, 41

PlayStation video game, 53-54

Renn, Veit, 31, 46
"Riddle" (single), 36
"Sailing" (single), 35
Spice Girls, 29, 34-35,
    39
"Tearin' Up My Heart"
    (single), 31, 32, 35
Timberlake, Justin

Randall, 7, 10, 20-
    23, 29, 34, 37, 40,
    47, 49, 52, 55, 57-
    58
Timberlake, Lynn,
    20-21, 26, 27, 28
"Together Again"
    (single), 36

"Trashin' the Camp"
    (soundtrack), 53
Truth Train, The
    (concert), 45
Wango Tango benefit,
    45
Wright, Jonny, 27-28,
    29, 31, 37

ABOUT THE AUTHOR

JOHN F. GRABOWSKI is a native of Brooklyn, New York. He holds a bachelor's degree in psychology from City College of New York and a master's degree in educational psychology from Teacher's College, Columbia University. He has been a teacher for 30 years, as well as a freelance writer, specializing in the fields of sports, education, and comedy. His body of published work includes 21 books; a nationally syndicated sports column; consultation on several math textbooks; articles for newspapers, magazines, and the programs of professional sports teams; and comedy material sold to Jay Leno, Joan Rivers, and numerous other comics. He and his wife, Patricia, live in Staten Island with their daughter, Elizabeth.

Unsolved Mysteries

Water Monsters

Brian Innes

RSVP
RAINTREE
STECK-VAUGHN
PUBLISHERS
A Steck-Vaughn Company

Austin, Texas

Developed by Brown Partworks
Editor: Lindsey Lowe
Designer: Joan Curtis

Raintree Steck-Vaughn Publishers Staff
Project Manager: Joyce Spicer
Editor: Pam Wells

Library of Congress Cataloging-in-Publication Data
Innes, Brian.
    Water monsters/by Brian Innes.
        p.   cm.—(Unsolved mysteries)
    Includes bibliographical references and index.
    Summary: Describes sightings of unidentified water creatures, including
the Biblical Leviathan, sea serpents, and the monsters supposedly inhabiting
various lakes.
    ISBN 0-8172-5479-X (Hardcover)
    ISBN 0-8172-4276-7 (Softcover)
    1. Marine animals—Juvenile literature. 2. Sea monsters—Juvenile literature.
[1. Sea monsters. 2. Monsters.] I. Title. II. Series: Innes, Brian. Unsolved
mysteries.
QL122.2.I56   1999
001.944—dc21   98-9353
                                                                 CIP
                                                                  AC
Printed and bound in the United States
1 2 3 4 5 6 7 8 9 0   WZ   02 01 00 99 98

Acknowledgments

Cover Norbert Wu/NHPA; **Page 5:** Charles
Walker Collection/Images Colour Library;
Page 6: Fortean Picture Library; **Page 7:** Stephen
Frink/Corbis; **Page 8:** Fortean Picture Library;
Page 9: Library of Congress/Corbis;
Page 11: Robert Le Serrec/Fortean Picture
Library; **Page 12:** James L. Amos/Corbis;
Pages 13 and 15: Fortean Picture Library;
Page 16: Kevin Schafer/Corbis; **Page 19:** Mary
Evans Picture Library; **Page 21:** Topham
Picturepoint; **Page 22:** Mary Evans Picture Library;
Page 23: Patrick Ward/Corbis; **Page 24:** Fortean
Picture Library; **Page 25:** Popperfoto;

Page 27: Nicholas Witchell/Fortean Picture
Library; **Page 29:** David Muench/Corbis;
Page 30: Fortean Picture Library; **Page 31:**
Kevin Morris/Corbis; **Page 33:** Hellin & Van
Ingen/NHPA; **Page 34:** Rene Dahinden/Fortean
Picture Library; **Page 37:** Rin Ergenbright/Corbis;
Page 38: Debbie Lee/Fortean Picture Library;
Page 39: Lars Thomas/Fortean Picture Library;
Page 41: Ivor Newby/Fortean Picture Library;
Page 43: Loren Coleman/Fortean Picture Library;
Page 44: Doug Perrine/Planet Earth Pictures;
Page 45: Pete Oxford/Planet Earth Pictures;
Page 46: Fortean Picture Library.

Contents

Creatures of the Deep   4

20th Century Sea Monsters   10

The Loch Ness Monster   20

The Lakes of North America   28

Lakes Around the World   36

Looking at the Evidence   42

Glossary   47

Index   48

Further Reading   48

Creatures of the Deep

Many years ago people thought monsters lived in the oceans. Do any still lurk in the murky depths?

For centuries, sailors have told tales of giant sea serpents. They have seen them all over the world. One sea monster, called Leviathan, is mentioned five times in the Bible. It is described as "the twisting serpent, the dragon that is in the sea."

Many stories of Leviathan were collected by Olaus Magnus, a Swedish archbishop. He lived more than 400 years ago. He described the creature as black with a mane and shining eyes. It raised its head "on high like a pillar." He said it was 200 feet (60 m) long, and 20 feet (6 m) thick. It ate calves, lambs, and hogs. It would even drag men from boats.

A BEAST KNOWN FROM LEGENDS

In the 18th century this description was confirmed. A Danish ship dropped its anchor in calm waters off the coast of West Africa. The captain, Jean-Magnus Dens, decided it was a good time to scrape the ship's hull. Men were lowered over the side on planks to do this.

Suddenly a monster rose out of the sea. It had enormous arms. It pulled two sailors into the water. A third arm seized another sailor.

The legend of the sea monster Leviathan (opposite) struck terror in the hearts of sailors for many centuries.

4

"It raised its head 'on high like a pillar' . . . . It ate calves, lambs, and hogs. It would even drag men from boats."

His shipmates saved him by hacking through the monster's arm. The monster sank out of sight. The captain measured the piece of arm. It was 25 feet (7.5 m) long, and covered with suckers. He thought the whole arm must have been nearly 40 feet (12 m) long!

MONSTROUS SQUIDS

Pierre Denys de Montfort believed Captain Dens's story. He was a French expert on mollusks, animals with no backbone, usually living in a shell. He began to follow up every story he heard about giant squids. In the 1790s he went to Dunkirk, in northern France. A group of American whaling ships was based there. He met with Ben Johnson, one of the captains. Johnson told De Montfort that part of a squid arm had been found in a whale's mouth. The arm was 35 feet (10.5 m) long. De Montfort guessed the full length of the arm must have been nearly 80 feet (24 m).

Then they shared another story. The crew of a slave ship had been off the coast of West Africa. Suddenly a huge squid surfaced. The tips of its arms reached as high as the masts. It pulled the ship over. The crew prayed to St. Thomas. They managed to cut off the monster's arms and save themselves. As a thanksgiving, the

In 1861, the crew of the French gunboat Alecton tried to pull the body of an enormous squid on board, but failed.

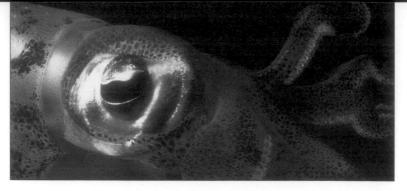

It is no wonder that early seafarers thought the oceans were full of monsters. Just the eye of a giant squid can be as much as 18 inches (46 cm) wide!

crew hung a painting of the incident in St. Thomas's chapel at St. Malo in France.

De Montfort hurried to St. Malo to look at the painting. Later he described it to an artist. The artist made a picture from the description. De Montfort took the picture to Paris, the capital city of France. But none of the scientists in Paris believed the story. People laughed at De Montfort's ideas. The painting later disappeared. It has never been seen again.

PRIZE CATCHES

Some 60 to 70 years later, De Montfort's findings did not look so funny. On November 30, 1861, the French gunboat *Alecton* was near Tenerife, in the Canary Islands. The lookout spotted the body of a huge squid floating on the water. The ship's commander wanted to land it. After many attempts, the crew got a rope around the squid. They tried to pull it on board the ship. But the squid broke into pieces. Most fell back into the water and were washed away.

Later, dead and dying squids began to wash up on the coasts of Canada. The biggest one on record in Canada was found on November 2, 1878. Its body was over 20 feet (6 m) long. One of its arms was 35 feet (10.5 m) long. Its suckers were 4 inches (10 cm) across. Its eyes were 18 inches (46 cm) wide.

In the late 20th century a giant male pink squid was caught off the coast of Peru. It also had arms 35 feet (10.5 m) long. Its eyes were over 1 foot (30 cm) wide. Biologists worked out the size of the whole squid from the pieces. It would have been over 100 feet (30 m) long. In 1997 a report in the *New York Times* told of a giant female squid that had been captured off the coast of Australia. It was 50 feet (15 m) long. The giant squid certainly exists.

This etching of the Gloucester sea serpent became well-known after the monster was first seen in June 1815

GIANT SNAKES

During the 18th and 19th centuries, many experienced naturalists kept an open mind about the existence of sea serpents. In the U.S., sea serpents were often spotted off the coast of New England. In June 1815, one was seen swimming rapidly through the water in Gloucester Bay, Massachusetts. It had a head like a horse and was dark brown. Its body was about 100 feet (30 m) long. It looked like a string of 30 to 40 humps, each the size of a barrel.

Judge Lonson Nash also said he saw the monster in Gloucester Bay. He led an investigation into all the sightings. This was organized by a group of New England scientists who studied living things. They decided the animal was a huge snake. They thought it had come to lay eggs on shore. No eggs were discovered, but two boys later found a creature. It was

"... it was 'just a black snake.'"

CHARLES-ALEXANDRE LESUEUR

3 feet (91 cm) long. It looked like a black snake, but it had humps on its back. Some thought it was a baby sea serpent. The biologists were excited. They named it *Scoliophis Atlanticus* (Atlantic Humped Snake). They cut it apart to examine it. But then a French zoologist, Charles-Alexandre Lesueur, looked at it. He said it was "just a black snake." Its spine had been deformed by injury or disease.

However, sightings of sea serpents continued. In 1820, the commander of the merchant ship *Lady Combermere* reported a serpent in the mid-Atlantic. It was 60 feet (18 m) long. In the 1830s, similar sightings of monsters were reported off Charleston, South Carolina, and Mahone Bay, Nova Scotia.

Most scientists laughed at such stories. However, reports of them have continued. Sea serpents are apparently still being sighted today.

Scientists in the 19th century laughed at reports of the existence of sea serpents. But does this 1906 photograph prove them right or wrong?

9

20th Century Sea Monsters

In the 20th century, photos finally proved the existence of sea monsters. Or did they?

Tales of strange creatures of the deep continued into the 20th century. Transatlantic passenger traffic was at its height during the 1920s and 1930s, and many people on cruises claimed to have seen sea monsters. There were also more reports of close-up sightings. There were even pictures to prove them!

CLOSE CONTACTS

For many years, a sea serpent had been seen in Chesapeake Bay, Maryland. Known locally as "Chessie," it became a film star in 1982. On May 21, Robert Frew and his wife, Karen, were entertaining guests at their home on Kent Island. Their home was near the north end of the vast bay. Around 7:00 P.M., they all saw Chessie. The sea serpent was in clear, shallow water about 200 yards (182 m) away. Robert grabbed his video camera. He began shooting film from an upper bedroom window.

The monster was moving up and down in the water. It was heading toward a party of swimmers. The Frews and their friends shouted. But the swimmers did not hear them. The swimmers did not notice the monster either. It dived

Before the 1960s, no monsters had been photographed clearly. Then, in 1965, Robert Le Serrec astonished the world with color pictures (opposite) that he had taken in Australia. They appeared to show sea monsters.

"It was shaped like an enormous tadpole. It had a big head, and a long, tapering body."

"Chessie" the sea serpent is said to lurk beneath the tranquil waters of Chesapeake Bay, Maryland.

underneath them, then surfaced on the far side of the bay. The creature was dark brown, and had a humpback. Those who saw it said it was about 35 feet (10.5 m) long and 1 foot (30 cm) thick. But it was only showing part of its body, so it could have been longer.

The videotape shot by Robert Frew ran for three minutes. Scientists hoped that it might prove the sea serpent's existence. An important meeting of seven experts was held at the Smithsonian Institution, in Washington, D.C. However, the pictures on the tape were blurred. There was not enough detail for any conclusion to be reached.

A SEA GIANT

On the other side of the Atlantic, there have been many sightings of a sea monster off Falmouth, in Cornwall, England. It has appeared close inshore. In the old Cornish language, the monster has been named "Morgawr," which means sea giant. It was seen in 1876, and twice early in the 20th century. Then, in 1976, "Mary F." produced photographs.

She said the part of the beast she saw was about 15 to 18 feet (4.5 to 5.4 m) long. It looked "like an elephant waving its trunk. But the trunk was a long neck, with a small head on the end, like a snake's head." It seemed to be humpbacked. Its humps moved "in a funny way." Its skin was dark brown,

or black, like a sea lion's. The photographs seemed genuine. But "Mary F." would not give her full name or address. Nor would she allow the negatives of the photos to be examined.

Since 1976, Morgawr has been sighted by many people. On July 10, 1985, author Sheila Bird was sitting on a cliff with her brother Eric, a scientist. Eric suddenly spotted a large, blotchy gray creature in the water below. It had a long neck, a small head, and its body was humpbacked. From high on the cliff, the pair could also see a long, muscled tail under the water. It was about the same length as the creature's body. The animal appeared to be nearly 20 feet (6 m) long. It held its head up high as it swam. Then it suddenly dived and disappeared.

SEA MONSTERS IN THE PACIFIC

Until late in the 19th century, there was little sea traffic in the Pacific Ocean. There were few tales of sea serpents. Also, there were no confirmed reports

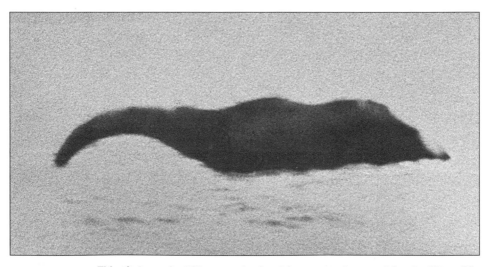

This photograph of Morgawr, the Cornish sea monster, was taken by "Mary F." in February 1976. Its long, slim neck and humpbacked body are clearly visible.

of monsters seen from the west coast of the United States until 1914. Then regular reports of a sea serpent began to come in. It had been seen swimming in the warm waters of the Outer Santa Barbara Channel, somewhere between the San Clemente and Santa Catalina islands, south of Los Angeles.

"I saw this great eel-like monster rear its head. Its eyes were red and green. . . ."

A. E. RICHARDS, FIRST OFFICER OF THE *SANTA LUCIA*

In 1920, Ralph Bandini, secretary of the Tuna Club, got a good look at it. It was truly a monster. Its head and neck rose 10 feet (3 m) out of the water. Bandini reckoned the neck was more than 5 feet (1.5 m) wide. The body was dark. It had a mane that looked like coarse hair. It also had huge, bulging eyes. Bandini thought that the monster was bigger than the largest whale.

Farther up the Pacific coast, near Vancouver in Canada, there was a monster known locally as "Caddy." This is short for Cadborosaurus. That name was jokingly given to it because it was most often seen in Cadboro Bay. On August 10, 1932, it was seen by F. W. Kemp, a local government official. It swam at amazing speed through the Strait of Georgia, between Vancouver Island and the British Columbia mainland.

In the following year, at dawn on October 21, 1933, the liner *Santa Lucia* was close to Cadboro Bay. First Officer A. E. Richards was on the bridge.

He reported: "I saw this great eel–like monster rear its head. Its eyes were red and green, like the port and starboard lights of a ship. It was about 90 feet [27 m] long. As we approached within 200 feet [60 m], it rose out of the water, with its seven humps like a camel, and its face like a cow. Then it gave an eerie [chilling] bellow—like a bull whale in its last agony—and reared up, perhaps 30 feet [9 m], perhaps 50 feet [15 m]. . . . By this time we had five searchlights on it, and it turned to the side and dived."

Caddy was seen often during the early 1930s. Then, on October 4, 1936, the skeleton of what was thought to be Caddy was found on some rocks off the coast of British Columbia. In spite of this, people in the area continued to report regular sightings of a monster resembling Caddy.

HUMPS AT SEA

On the afternoon of October 31, 1983, a road crew was repairing a stretch of U.S. Highway 1 in Marin County, California. The stretch where they were

Was this the skeleton of Caddy? The bones were found on the rocks at Camp Fircom, off the coast of British Columbia, on October 4, 1936.

working runs along the coast north of San Francisco Bay. One of the crew, Matt Ratto, saw something very large traveling fast through the water toward the shore. It was a huge, dark animal. It was just a quarter of a mile (400 m) away. Ratto said it was 100 feet (30 m) long. But it was quite thin, "like a long black eel." He counted three humps. Then the creature turned and swam out to sea.

Truck driver Steve Bjora thought it moved at 45–50 miles per hour (mph) (72–80 kilometers per hour [kmph]). He saw only two humps. Altogether, five members of the construction crew saw the beast. They agreed on its appearance. Transportation safety inspector Marlene Martin also observed it. But she refused to talk about it. However, her daughter said her mother had told her she saw four humps. It was the largest thing she had ever seen.

This is San Francisco Bay. On October 31, 1983, many people witnessed a large beast traveling fast through the still waters toward the shore.

Three days later, a similar creature was seen. This time a group of surfers saw it. They were more than 400 miles (640 km) to the south, near Costa Mesa. Young Hutchinson described how it rose up out of the water. It was just off the Santa Ana River jetty. And that was only 10 feet (3 m) from his surfboard. He, too, said nothing at first. He thought "the whole thing was too crazy." Then he read about the Marin County sightings. His description was similar—a long, black eel.

PHOTOGRAPHIC EVIDENCE

Before the 1960s, nobody had taken a photograph of a sea monster. Until then, biologists had to rely on the descriptions of eyewitnesses. They really wanted to study a living creature, but a good picture would help. In 1965 a French photographer, Robert Le Serrec, claimed to have one.

On December 12, 1964, said Le Serrec, he was in a boat off the coast of Queensland, Australia. With him were his family and a friend named Henk de Jong. They were crossing the shallow waters of Stonehaven Bay. Suddenly Le Serrec's wife spotted something huge on the sandy seabed. It was only 6 feet (2 m) below. At first, the party thought it was a big, sunken tree trunk. Then, they realized it was an animal. It was shaped like an enormous tadpole. It had a big head and a long, tapering body.

Le Serrec took several photographs (see page 11). He moved closer. He began to film with his movie camera. Now the boat was nearer. The party could see the huge head more clearly. It was shaped like a snake's. Down the animal's back was a big wound, some 5 feet (1.5 m) long. The children in the boat

17

were frightened. They were taken back to shore. The adults went back to look at the monster. It did not move. So they guessed it was either dead or injured. They got even closer. They could see two white eyes on top of the head. There were bands of brown all along its black body.

"The monster began to move its jaws. It looked as if it was going to harm them."

Le Serrec later claimed he had a special camera with him to film the creature underwater. He and de Jong decided to dive near the animal for a closer look. But the water was cloudier than they thought. They had to swim to within 20 feet (6 m) of the beast. They judged its length to be about 75–80 feet (23–24 m). Its mouth was 4 feet (1 m) wide. The eyes were about 2 inches (5 cm) across. Now that Le Serrec and de Jong were close, they saw that the eyes were not white, but pale green. Le Serrec began filming. The monster began to move its jaws. It looked as if it was going to harm them. They quickly swam back to the boat. There Le Serrec's wife told them the monster had swum out to sea.

THE WORLD WONDERS

The Frenchman released his story on February 4, 1965. It created great excitement. However, there were some who refused to believe it. The photos seemed genuine. But few people were allowed to see the movies. It was rumored that they were blurred

and almost useless. Then some damaging facts about Le Serrec began to surface. He was wanted by the international police organization called Interpol.

In 1960 Le Serrec had left France, taking money he had been lent for an expedition. He told the people who lent him the money that he had an idea to make their fortune. He said the idea had "to do with a sea serpent." Le Serrec was arrested when he returned to France in 1966. He spent six months in jail. His photos appeared in the magazine *Paris Match*. But later, another publication revealed they had been a trick!

A decade later another photograph excited the scientists. On April 10, 1977, the fishing trawler *Zuiyo Maru* was off Christchurch, New Zealand. The crew found the body of a huge animal in one of their nets. It was decaying and stank. The crew was worried it would contaminate the catch of fish. They took photographs of it. It was also measured. The body was then thrown back into the sea. However, biologists later analyzed the information. They said the body was probably that of a large basking shark. Could all sea monsters simply be basking sharks or other fish?

A slightly fanciful drawing of a basking shark done in 1804. A similar creature could have been what the crew of Zuiyo Maru *caught in its nets in 1977.*

The Loch Ness Monster

"Nessie" is the most famous water monster in the world. But its identity remains a mystery.

Loch Ness is a long, narrow lake in the Great Glen, which cuts like a deep canyon across the Highlands of Scotland. The loch is 22 miles (35 km) long. It is more than 970 feet (297 m) deep, but it is less than 1 mile (1.6 km) wide.

The first known sighting of the Loch Ness monster was 1,500 years ago. St. Columba had set up a monastery on the island of Iona, off Scotland's west coast. From there, he traveled through the north of Scotland. His task was to preach Christianity.

A LUCKY ESCAPE

In 565, St. Columba came to Loch Ness. One of his followers, called Lugne, was bold enough to swim across the mouth of the Ness River. He wanted to take a boat from the other side. Suddenly he met a "very odd looking beastie, something like a huge frog, only it was not a frog." The monster opened its mouth. It swam to attack Lugne.

Seeing this, St. Columba raised his arms and shouted: "Go thou no farther, nor touch the man. Go back at once!" Then, according to the account, "on hearing this word, the monster

There have been countless sightings of "Nessie," and many photographs have been shot. One of the best was taken by Jennifer Bruce in 1982 (opposite).

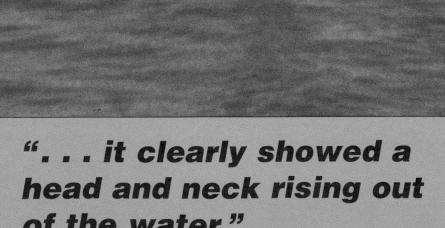

". . . it clearly showed a head and neck rising out of the water."

was terrified and fled away again. . . ."

In Scotland, the monster was called "Niseag." This is a Scottish Gaelic word. Its English name was "Nessie." For centuries, local people lived in fear of the monster. Children were told not to play near the water. There were hundreds of descriptions of the beast.

St. Columba, who lived from 521 to 597, traveled through the north of Scotland preaching Christianity. In 565, he arrived at Loch Ness and saw the monster.

Patrick Rose reported, in 1771, that he had seen something in the loch. He described it as half like a horse, and half like a camel. In 1880, Duncan McDonald was trying to raise a sunken boat. "I was underwater about my work," he said, "when all of a sudden the monster swam by me as cool and calm as you please." In 1907, a group of children saw Nessie. She was slipping into the water. They said the monster had four legs. She was light brown in color. She looked "like a camel."

FRESH SIGHTINGS

For a few years, all seemed to be quiet. Then, on July 22, 1930, a man called Ian Milne was fishing for salmon with two friends.

They were in a small boat. Some 600 yards (546 m) away they suddenly saw spray being thrown high up into the air. A creature rushed toward them. It turned, then moved away again. It traveled at a speed of some 15 mph (24 kmph). "The part of it

we saw would be about 20 feet [6 m] long. And it was standing 3 feet [60 cm] or so out of the water. The wash [waves] it created caused our boat to rock violently," reported Milne.

Until the 1930s the shores of Loch Ness were difficult to reach. Then, a new road was built along the north shore. Tourists began to arrive. Soon Nessie made the newspaper headlines. In spring, 1933, John Mackay and his wife told the *Inverness Courier* they had seen the monster for a minute or more. Mackay said the beast made the water "froth and foam." It had a very small head when compared to the size of its body.

Three months later, on July 22, George Spicer and his wife were driving along the new road. Their car nearly hit a huge black beast with a long neck. It waddled through the undergrowth. Then, it went into the water. Later the same year, on November 12, Hugh Gray was standing by the loch. He saw something large rise out of the water. So he took a photograph of it. He guessed it was 40 feet (12 m) long. He said it was gray, and had a very smooth, shiny skin.

This was the first photograph ever to have been taken of Nessie. It was printed in newspapers all over the world. However, it was very blurred.

The following year, on April 12, a clearer photograph appeared.

Castle Urquhart once stood alone on the shores of Loch Ness. When a new road was built close by, tourists arrived—and sightings of Nessie began to increase.

23

It was taken by a London physician, Colonel Robert Wilson. The picture showed a creature with a big body, a long neck, and a small head. Nessie looked like the ancient water reptile known as a plesiosaur.

STALKING THE MONSTER

Rewards were offered for the capture of Nessie. However, scientific experts were skeptical. At the British Museum, J. R. Norman stated: "The possibilities came down to the object being a bottlenose whale, one of the large species of shark, or just mere wreckage." He did not explain how a whale or shark could have gotten into Loch Ness.

World War II broke out in 1939. People had other things to think about. It was not until the 1950s that Nessie became news again. One of those who reported a sighting was David Slorach. He described it to *Harper's* magazine. On February 4, 1954, he was driving along the north shore of Loch Ness to Inverness. What he saw reminded him of "a cat with a long neck. One black floppy 'ear' fell

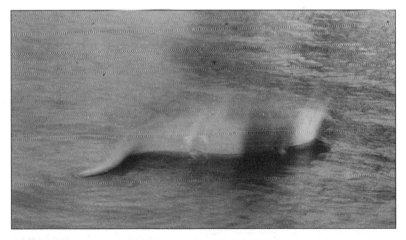

Hugh Gray took this photograph on November 12, 1933. It was the first photograph of Nessie, and it appeared in newspapers all over the world.

This is one of the clearest early photographs of Nessie. It was taken on April 12, 1934, by Colonel Robert Wilson. Experts say it resembles a plesiosaur—an ancient water reptile.

over where the eye might be, and four long black streaks ran down the 'neck.' The object was traveling through the water at great speed, throwing up a huge wave behind."

A special "Loch Ness Investigation Bureau" was set up. Then, in 1960 and 1967, the monster was caught on film. Both films were blurred, but showed a fast-moving object leaving a wave behind it as it shot through the water. Experts suggested that this was caused by an otter. But the object's length above the loch's surface was about 7 feet (2.1 m). This was much longer than any otter.

STRANGE SHAPES

On the evening of May 4, 1968, a number of people sighted what they thought was the monster. In August, a team from Birmingham University, England, set up a sonar scanner on a pier in Loch Ness. A sonar scanner is a machine that detects any sound made by moving objects. On August 28, they made a remarkable 13-minute recording.

A large object rose through the water from the bottom of the loch. It was about half a mile (800 m) away from them. It was traveling at a speed of around 100 feet (30 m) per minute, moving away from the pier. Then the object turned toward the

pier again and dived deep. The sounds from a second object were recorded at the same time. This object dived at 450 feet (135 m) per minute.

"... if there is a monster, or more than one, in Loch Ness, what can it be?"

The leader of the scientific team, Dr. Braithwaite, wrote that the rapid speeds that had been recorded for both objects made it unlikely that they were schools of fish, which had been one possible explanation. And in any case, biologists were unable to suggest what type of fish they might have been.

FILMING NESSIE

It was not until 1970 that underwater photography was tried. Because the water was murky, this was difficult. But there were some interesting results. Dr. Robert Rines, a scientific expert from Boston, Massachusetts, was one of the most successful. He took photographs that showed some kind of animal fin. Later, something that looked like a complete long-necked creature was photographed.

Above water, visitors to Loch Ness continued to produce photographs they claim are of the monster surfacing. One of the most convincing was taken by Jennifer Bruce in 1982. She took a picture of the view across part of the loch. At the time she noticed nothing unusual. But, when the photograph was developed, it clearly showed a head and neck rising out of the water.

A MYSTERIOUS IDENTITY

If there is a monster, or more than one, in Loch Ness, what can it be? Most descriptions are closest to that of a plesiosaur—a water reptile believed to have been extinct for the past 70 million years. Animals are said to be extinct, meaning that they have all died, once they have not been seen for a long time. But they may still exist. Until 1938, the coelacanth, a very ugly fish, was also said to have been extinct for 70 million years. Then fishermen started catching it in the Indian Ocean.

OPERATION DEEPSCAN

Nessielike monsters have also been reported in nearby lochs. Whatever these beasts are, teams of people continue to seek them. Between 1962 and 1977, six different groups of people used the most modern equipment to explore Loch Ness. They obtained results that could not be explained as being due to fish, nor anything like a sunken log.

Then, in 1987, came "Operation Deepscan." A fleet of motorboats, each equipped with sound-detecting equipment, swept the loch from end to end. But they found nothing. That was not really surprising. The boats filled the area with the noise of their engines. That would surely frighten any creature into hiding. So the search for Nessie continues.

In 1987, "Operation Deepscan" attempted to solve the Loch Ness mystery. However, the fleet of 24 boats failed to find any trace of Nessie.

The Lakes of North America

It is not just the lochs of Scotland that have monsters. The lakes of North America have them too!

One of the most famous lake monsters of North America is "Champ." It haunts Lake Champlain—a narrow lake like Loch Ness, but much longer. It runs for 109 miles (175 km) due south from the Canadian border, between New York State and Vermont.

The traditional story is that the monster was spotted in 1609 by French explorer Samuel de Champlain. The lake bears his name. But the first record of Champ's being seen was made in the summer of 1819. A boatman reported that he saw a huge creature with a long neck. It held its head 15 feet (4.5 m) above the water. At first, many people doubted the truth of the story. However, there have been some 250 sightings of Champ since then.

Lake Champlain (opposite) is 109 miles (175 km) long. It provides an enormous playground for "Champ," one of North America's most famous monsters.

THE DEFINITIVE DESCRIPTION

The first detailed description of the Champlain monster came in July 1883. It was given by Captain Nathan H. Mooney, the sheriff of Clinton County, New York. He was on the northwest shore of the lake when he saw an enormous "water serpent" rise out of the water. It was about 50 yards (46 m) away. Its head

"A boatman reported that he saw a huge creature with a long neck."

appeared 5 feet (1.5 m) above the rough waves. He figured that its neck was about 7 inches (18 cm) thick, and he put the full length of the body at 25–30 feet (8–9 m). He said the neck was curved, "like a goose when about to take flight." He could see strong muscles in the creature's neck. And he noted round white spots inside its mouth.

A STAR IS BORN

Numerous reports were made over many years. Then, in July 1981, the little village of Port Henry, New York, at the southern end of the lake, decided to exploit the fame of the monster. Buildings were painted apple green because the villagers had decided that this was the color of the monster. The names of 100 people who had sighted Champ were painted on a wooden billboard. This was posted at the entrance to Port Henry

Then pictures of a cartoon-like beast appeared in the shop windows and on signposts. There were even T-shirts and special buttons.

This drawing, from the book Historia Canadensis (1664), is the monster Samuel de Champlain saw In the lake in 1609.

In the late summer of 1981, the *New York Times* printed a photograph taken four years earlier by Mrs. Sandra Mansi of Connecticut. It showed a dark body, with a long neck lifted clear of the water. Mrs. Mansi said she thought it looked "like a dinosaur." The photograph appeared to be real. Sadly the negative has been lost.

Monsters have been seen in other lakes: Flathead Lake, Montana; Lake Walker, Nevada; Lake Folsom, California; Bear Lake, Utah; and Lake Payette, Idaho.

Lake Payette, Idaho, is home to Slimy Slim. The monster has been spotted at different times by more than 30 people.

In July and August 1941, "Slimy Slim" was spotted in Lake Payette by more than 30 different people. For a time afterward, nobody reported the sightings. Then Thomas L. Rogers, city auditor from Boise, Idaho, spoke to a local newspaper reporter.

Rogers said the serpent was about 50 feet (15 m) long. It moved with a wavy motion at about 5 mph (8 kmph). He said its head was like that of a snubnosed crocodile. It was about 8 inches (20 cm) above the water. He figured the total length of the body at about 35 feet (10.5 m). The story of Slimy Slim was published in *Time* magazine, but after that little was seen or heard of it again.

CANADIAN MONSTERS

There are said to be monsters in many of the lakes of the St. Lawrence River valley, north of the Canadian border. Lake Pohénégamook, in Quebec, close by the border with Maine, has its "Ponik." The town of Saint-Eleuthére, at the head of the lake, holds a regular "Ponik festival." Sightings have been reported since 1873.

Father Calixte Bérubé, a priest, has described what he and 15 other people saw one afternoon. "From the path, we had a magnificent view of the lake. We saw the back with its fin. It frolicked like a fish and shimmered in the sun." In the mid-1970s, three divers spent 10 days searching for Ponik. They took a picture of a dark shape some 25 feet (8 m) long.

Farther south, crossing from Canada into the state of Maine, lies Lake Memphremagog. This is another narrow lake some 50 miles (80 km) long.

On October 26, 1935, Dr. Curtis Classen, from Brooklyn, New York, was staying at his vacation home beside the lake. His back was to the water when he sensed something staring at him. Turning,

"It frolicked like a fish and shimmered in the sun."

FATHER CALIXTE BÉRUBÉ

he saw a creature like a large alligator. It was climbing onto the bank. He ran to bring his wife and a friend. They were just in time to see the creature crawling back into the water. There were large pawprints on the sandy shore.

In a letter written later, Dr. Classen said: "We estimated [guessed] that the creature was 18 inches [46 cm] wide and 10 feet [3 m] long." In October 1937, John Webster also saw prints on the same beach. He figured the animal that left them had been about 20 inches (51 cm) wide and 11 feet (3 m) long. In 1966 or 1967, Hank Dewey was fishing on the lake with two women passengers. Suddenly "a big fish, but it did not look like a fish," appeared near the bank. "The women were so frightened that they never again went on the lake."

SCALED TERROR
A very different description of the monster of Lake Memphremagog was given in 1972. It was about 10:00 P.M. on a clear night. Mrs. Helen Hicks was

in a small boat with an outboard motor. A spotlight from the boat fell on the creature. Mrs. Hicks said the creature was about 75–100 feet (23–30 m) long. It had a round body. Its head was like that of a horse, with two red eyes. The neck was long. And the back appeared to be covered with large scales. "It started to come for the boat. It rolled over near the boat, causing it to be very tippy. It shorted out the boat motor."

Some experts believe many of the monsters of the Canadian lakes are really giant sturgeons. These fish, they say, can grow up to 12 feet (3.6 m) long. But the monsters could also be a type of dinosaur—the lakes of Canada and Alaska are left over from the last ice age. Perhaps there are all sorts of creatures, trapped in the water, that have yet to be discovered.

THE SNAKE IN THE LAKE

Of all the North American monsters, the most famous is probably Ogopogo. This monster is said to inhabit Lake Okanagan, a long, deep, mountain lake in British Columbia. Native Americans told

Although this may look like a monster, it is not! It is a giant sturgeon that lives in the fresh waters of some Canadian lakes. Many experts believe that this is what people have seen when they claim to have spotted a monster.

tales of Naitaka, "snake of the water." When they had to cross the lake, they would throw in live animals to satisfy it.

In the 1850s, John MacDougall was crossing Lake Okanagan in his canoe. Two horses were swimming behind on ropes. He forgot about the monster, and the need to feed it. Suddenly, something began to pull a horse down. It would have dragged the canoe under. But MacDougall cut the ropes with his knife, leaving the horses to their fate.

OGOPOGO REVEALS ITSELF

In July 1890, Captain Thomas Shorts, of the steamer *Jubilee*, saw a creature some 15 feet (4.5 m) long. It had a head like a ram. The sun shone through its fins. This was the first reported sighting. Soon there were others. They continued year after year.

In the summer of 1952, a woman visitor from Vancouver saw the monster. It was swimming just a couple of hundred yards away. She said later: "I am a stranger here. I didn't even know such things existed. But I saw it so plainly. A head like a cow, or a horse, that reared right out of the water. It was a wonderful sight. The coils glistened like two huge wheels. There were ragged edges along its back, like a saw. It was so beautiful, with the sun shining on it."

In August 1968, Art Folden and his wife were driving home along the shore of the lake. They suddenly noticed something moving in the water. It

A model of Ogopogo (Lake Okanagan's monster) at Kelowna, British Columbia.

was about 300 yards (273 m) away. Folden had a small movie camera with him. It was loaded with color film and had a telephoto lens. He had been using it to film the day's outing. Fortunately there were a few feet of film left.

Folden shot film for about one minute, in short bursts. He photographed the object only when it was visible on the surface. This was an important sighting. But Folden kept quiet about it. He showed his film only to friends and relatives. Then, in February 1970, his brother-in-law persuaded him to show it to other people. It caused a sensation.

Judging from the size of the pine trees in the foreground, the creature was about 60 feet (18 m) long, and 3 feet (90 cm) wide. It moved very fast and left a clear wake. Some people thought they could see a head and tail. Others were not so sure. However, local author Arlene Gaal was convinced by the film. She had studied the Ogopogo reports for years. In 1981 she herself took a photograph of something she believed was the monster.

WAS IT A BEAVER?

In 1989 Ken Chaplin shot a video of something moving through the water. He described it as a dark green, snakelike creature. He said it was about 15 feet (4.5 m) long. Wildlife experts were shown the video. However, they thought the animal was more likely a beaver, or a large otter.

Hunting guide Ernie Giroux saw a creature close to the same spot. Giroux was told what the experts had made of Chaplin's video. "I've seen a lot of animals swimming in the wild," he said, "and what we saw that night was definitely not a beaver."

35

Lakes Around the World

There are lakes the world over. And many are home to strange creatures.

One of the first tales of lake monsters in South America was told by Father Juan-Ignacio Molina. In his *Essay on the Natural History of Chile*, published in 1782, he wrote that the natives of Chile reported "a fish or dragon of monstrous size." They called it the "fox-serpent." They believed it ate people, so they never swam in the lakes where it lived.

SUMMER SIGHTINGS

Close to Chile, in the Andean mountains of southern Argentina, lies Lake Nahuel Huapi. It covers 380 square miles (984 sq km). Here a monster has been seen by many visitors, as well as by local people. Nicknamed "Nahuelito," it seems to surface only in summer. That may be because summer is the tourist season.

Nahuelito appears when the lake is calm. There is a sudden swell and a shooting spray of water. Descriptions of the creature vary greatly. Its length has been said to be anything from 15 to 150 feet (4.5 to 45 m). Some witnesses have reported a giant water snake with humps, and fins like a fish. Others describe it as "a swan with a snake's head."

An approaching storm whips up the waters of Lake Nahuel Huapi (opposite) in Argentina. It is only during the summer months that its monster, "Nahuelito," makes an appearance.

" 'Nahuelito' appears when the lake is calm. There is a sudden swell and a shooting spray of water."

On the other side of the world, in the African Republic of Congo, people tell stories of monsters called mokele-mbembe. These are terrifying creatures, the size of a hippopotamus. But the mokele-mbembe has a long neck and tail, and clawed feet. It is said to attack canoes, killing all aboard.

PREHISTORIC LANDSCAPE

Scientist Roy Mackal decided to brave the danger. In 1980 and 1981 he mounted searches for the monster. The explorers plunged into the Likouala swamp. This is a huge, almost unexplored area of the Republic of Congo, on the border with the Central African Republic. Crammed into a dugout canoe, the party searched the waterways of the swamp. It was like parts of the world had been when the dinosaurs roamed, millions of years ago. Perhaps mokele-mbembe was a survivor from those times.

An officer of the Congolese Army told Mackal that the creature dug caves in the banks of the waterways. Mackal was shown mokele-mbembe's footprint. But he was forced to admit that this might have been made by an elephant. And as for the creature itself, there was not a trace.

Throughout parts of Europe there are many reports of a monster known as a "water-horse." This

This painting of mokele-mbembe was based on eyewitness descriptions of those who had seen the monster in Africa.

comes out from a lake or river. Then, according to legend, it carries men, women, and children away. People in the U.S. and Canada have also reported monsters with a mane, or a head like a horse. It seems likely that they are describing a similar animal.

NORTHERN EUROPE

One of these monsters is said to live in Lake Storsjön, in central Sweden. It has been reported for more than 350 years. A century ago, a scientist named Dr. Peter Olsson spent many years following up sightings. The beast was red, with a white mane. It

In the 1970s, a huge trap (above) was made in Sweden. It was baited with baby pigs. Then it was put beside Lake Storsjön. But the monster did not take the bait.

moved very fast, at a speed of some 45 mph (72 kmph). Since 1987, nearly 500 different sightings have been recorded. Some witnesses have described a beast with a long neck. The movement of its neck looks like the waving of a horse's mane. Others reported that the creature was like a giant worm. But it had ears on its head. Estimates of its length vary from 10–45 feet (3–14 m).

Iceland also has its monster. English author Reverend Sabine Baring-Gould visited that country in 1860. He was told about the monster "Skrimsl." It lived in the lake called Lagarfljot. The monster was 50 feet (15 m) long. In Norway, he heard about a similar creature in Lake Suidal. Its head was said to be

as big as a rowboat. More than a century later, in August 1986, Aasmund Skori observed something in Norway's Lake Seljord. The water was calm, and he saw a sort of "bow" emerge. "The bow was one and a half meters [5 feet] long," he said, "as thick as a thigh, and looked black. The body divided the water in front. Behind it the lake was frothing."

"The monster looked like a horse. But it had big eyes and a forked tail."

THE WATER-HORSE IN IRELAND

The greatest number of stories about the "water-horse" come from Ireland. The name usually given to the beast in Irish is "peiste." One of the earliest descriptions is in the 10th century *Book of Lismore*. The monster looked like a horse. But it had big eyes and a forked tail. The 12th century *Book of the Dun Cow* tells of a peiste living in the deep lake of Slieve Mis, in County Kerry. It would come out of the water to seize cattle.

In the 19th and 20th centuries, monsters were reported from a number of the lakes of Connemara, in County Galway. As in Canada, these lakes were formed at the end of the last ice age. There are hundreds of these lakes—known in Ireland as "loughs"—dotted all over the land.

On February 22, 1968, farmer Stephen Coyne was on the shores of Lough Nahooin. He saw something black in the water. He thought it was his dog. So he whistled. The shape in the water did not respond.

Then, to his surprise, his dog came running up to him from behind. When it saw the creature in the lough, it began barking.

Coyne was joined by his wife and children. They watched the monster for some time, until the light faded. It came to within 30 feet (9 m) of them. It was about 12 feet (4 m) long. It had a smooth skin, like an eel. Its neck was 12 inches (30 cm) in diameter. The inside of its mouth was pale. When the monster put its head under the water, two humps appeared above the surface. They also saw its tail.

LEAVING THE WATER

Most of the great lakes where monsters have been reported—such as Lake Nahuel Huapi—are huge. But most of the loughs in Connemara are very small. There is not enough food in any one lough for a huge creature to live on. However, a creature might survive by leaving the water to seek food.

On September 8, 1968, farmer Thomas Connelly saw a black creature, "bigger than a young donkey," on the shore of Lough Nahooin. This lough is only 300 feet (91 m) long and 240 feet (73 m) wide. The black creature had four stumpy legs. It crept back into the water. If beasts such as this can move on dry land, then it would be possible for them to travel from one lough to another in search of food.

Monster hunting on Lough Nahooin in 1968. On the right is Roy Mackal, the U.S. scientist who later led the search for mokele-mbembe in Africa.

41

Looking at the Evidence

Mistaken identity probably accounts for most reported water monsters. But what about the rest?

Reports of monsters all around the world have created a new word—"cryptozoologist." The "crypto" part of the word means "hidden," and zoologists study animals. So cryptozoologists try to make sense of reports of animals unknown to everyday science.

One man, in particular, has spent many years analyzing the accounts of sea monsters. He is Dr. Bernard Heuvelmans, a Belgian zoologist. In 1965, he published his book *In the Wake of the Sea Serpents*. Here he listed studies of 587 events. The reports dated from 1639 to 1964.

SORTING THE SIGHTINGS

Out of his total of 587, Heuvelmans found 56 to be pretended sightings, or tricks. He decided that another 52 were sightings of known sea creatures—such as the giant squid. These creatures had been mistakenly described as unknown monsters. He put aside another 121 reports—the detail was too confused.

This left 358 sightings that Heuvelmans felt were real. He found that these could be divided into nine different types of animals: the long-necked; the merhorse (sea horse); the

The plesiosaur (opposite) is an ancient water reptile that existed when dinosaurs roamed the Earth over 150 million years ago.

42

"The descriptions of these creatures are like the prehistoric plesiosaur."

many-humped; the many-finned; the super-otter; the super-eel; the marine saurian (a reptile); the father-of-all-turtles; and the yellow-belly.

The creature most often reported is the long-necked sea serpent. The merhorse (sea horse) has a different-shaped head, more like that of a horse. It has big eyes and a red mane. The many-humped sea serpent and the super-otter are about the

The largest known species of turtle is the leatherback, which can measure 12 feet (4 m) across. It is possible that larger turtles exist.

same size, 60–100 feet (18–30 m) long. The many-humped serpent is the one that is most often seen along the coast of New England. It swims with a single pair of large fins. It also has a "forked" tail, like that of a shark. The super-otter has a thicker neck and a bigger head. It has a pair of big paws in front, and a pair of smaller paws, or fins, farther back.

FIGHTING FOR LIFE

Heuvelmans believed that the super-otter had not been sighted since 1848. He believed it was now extinct. He suggested that the long-necked sea serpent and the super-otter were competitors, and that the super-otter had probably lost the battle for survival. The many-finned monster grows to 60 feet (18 m) or more in length. It blows a spray of water from its nostrils, like a surfacing whale. It has only been sighted in tropical waters.

Heuvelmans believes the first five types of monsters are mammals. The super-eel is more likely to be a

fish. It normally lives deep in the ocean. It only comes to the surface when it is near death. The marine saurian is a reptile. It looks like a crocodile and has been seen only in tropical waters. It is 50–60 feet (15–18 m) long. It might be a survivor from Jurassic times, when dinosaurs roamed the earth more than 150 million years ago.

HARDY SURVIVORS

Turtles have been around for some 175 million years. The largest known type of turtle, called the Atlantic leatherback, can weigh more than three-quarters of a ton. It measures 12 feet (4 m) across. So it is possible that an animal like the "father-of-all-turtles" still lives in the warm tropical depths.

The "yellow-belly" is the most difficult to explain. There are few detailed descriptions. It may be a huge fish or an unknown species of shark.

Other cryptozoologists have made different suggestions. One of these is that the sea serpent is an unknown giant species, similar to the long-necked leopard seal of the Antarctic. Another is that it is a primitive or early type of whale called a zeuglodon, which is supposed to be extinct.

Many experts believe that the sea serpent could be a giant relation of the long-necked leopard seal that is found in the Antarctic (above).

PREHISTORIC ORIGINS

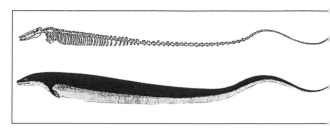

The zeuglodon is a primitive whale thought to have died out 50 million years ago. Perhaps the lake monsters "Champ," "Caddy," and "Ogopogo" are its survivors.

Many descriptions of water monsters sound like the prehistoric plesiosaur. However, most reports of such sightings are from the 20th century. Today most people know what prehistoric dinosaurs looked like. One description of a monster could well be a description of a plesiosaur. It looked like "a snake that had swallowed a barrel." But experts believe that the plesiosaur moved very slowly. Besides, its neck was not flexible. It could not move in the way witnesses have described.

Those who do not believe in water monsters have many explanations to offer. The most popular is that the "humps" of a sea serpent, moving fast through the sea, are really a line of porpoises jumping out of the water, one behind the other. And it has been suggested that the Loch Ness sightings are of a number of salmon, doing the same thing.

A BASIC EXPLANATION

Many people think that water monsters are nothing more than floating tree trunks. But this does not account for the rapid movement that so many witnesses report. Nothing will be known for sure until a monster is captured.

Huge areas of the Earth's surface remain largely unexplored. Many of these areas are in the oceans. Every year a thousand or more new species of living creatures are identified. Who knows when a new monster may emerge from the deep?

46

Glossary

archbishop An important priest in the Christian church.

biologists People who study biology, which is the science of living things.

bulging Swelling where you would expect something to be flat.

confirm (ed) To support or prove that something is correct.

contaminate To pollute or infect, or to make radioactive.

estimated The roughly worked out size, length, weight, or volume of something.

existence To be living, or real, rather than something from the imagination or in a story.

extinct No longer alive, active, or in existence.

fanciful Something from the imagination, often unrealistic.

ice age A time when Earth was covered with ice. There have been several ice ages in Earth's history.

incident A specific event.

jetty A platform built out into the water. Used for getting on and off boats, or to protect against the sea.

kmph Kilometers per hour.

mollusks Small creatures with no backbone. They have a soft body, and a hard shell—like a snail.

monstrous Enormous or huge, sometimes terrifying or bizarre.

mph Miles per hour.

naturalist A person who studies wildlife—animals and plants.

prehistoric Before humans began to keep written historical records.

resemble To look like, or behave like, something or somebody else.

skeptical To be unwilling to believe a claim or promise made by somebody else.

sonar scan A machine that detects sounds made by moving objects.

species Groups of plants or animals that have common features.

squids Sea creatures with long, soft bodies and 10 tentacles, or arms. An octopus has eight arms.

tapering Gradually narrowing.

trawler A type of boat that is used to catch fish at sea. Fish are caught in a trawl, a large bag-shaped net.

undergrowth The thick growth of bushes, shrubs, and other plants under trees in a wood or forest.

zoologist A person who studies zoology, the science of animals.

Index

"Caddy" (sea monster), 14–15, 46

"Champ" (lake monster), 28–30, 46

"Chessie" (sea serpent), 10, 12

cryptozoologists, 42

dinosaurs, 33, 42, 46

father-of-all-turtles (sea monster), 44, 45

fox-serpent (lake monster), 36

Lake Champlain monster *see* "Champ"

Lake Lagarfljot monster *see* "Skrimsl"

Lake Memphremagog monster, 32–33

lake monsters, 28–41, 46 *see also* Loch Ness Monster

Lake Nahuel Huapi monster *see* "Nahuelito"

Lake Okanagan monster *see* "Ogopogo"

Lake Payette monster *see* "Slimy Slim"

Lake Pohénégamook monster *see* "Ponik"

Lake Seljord monster, 40

Lake Storsjön monster, 39

Lake Suidal monster, 39–40

leatherback turtles, 44, 45

Leviathan (sea monster), 4–6

Loch Ness monster, 20–27, 46

Lough Nahooin monster, 40–41

many-finned monsters, 44

marine saurians (sea monsters), 44, 45

merhorses (sea monsters), 42, 44

mokele-mbembe (lake monster), 38

"Morgawr" (sea monster), 12–13

"Nahuclito" (lake monster), 36–37

"Nessie" or "Niscag" *see* Loch Ness monster

"Ogopogo" (lake monster), 33–35, 46

peistes (Irish water-horses), 40

plesiosaurs, 27, 42, 43, 46

"Ponik" (lake monster), 31

saurians, marine (sea monsters), 44, 45

Scoliophis Atlanticus (sea serpent), 9

sea monsters, 4–19, 46 types, 42, 44–45

sea serpents, 8–9, 10, 12, 13–17, 44, 45, 46

sharks, basking, 19

"Skrimsl" (lake monster), 39–40

"Slimy Slim" (lake monster), 30–31

squids, giant, 6–8, 42

sturgeons, giant, 33

super-eels (sea monsters), 44–45

super-otters (sea monsters), 44

turtles, 44, 45

water-horses (lake monsters), 38–39, 40–41

yellow-belly (sea monster), 44, 45

zeuglodons, 45, 46

Further Reading

Collard, Sneed B. *Sea Snakes*. Boyds Mills Press, 1997

Garcia, Eulalia. *Giant Squid: Monsters of the Deep*, "Secrets of the Animal World" series. Gareth Stevens, 1997

Landau, Elaine. *The Loch Ness Monster*, "Mysteries of Science" series. Millbrook Press, 1993

Ross, Stewart. *Monsters of the Deep*, "Fact or Fiction" series. Millbrook Press, 1997